TRIVQUIZ

1001
TRIVIA QUESTIONS
MANCHESTER
UNITED

FASCINATING FACTS! TRIVIA BRAINTEASERS!
WRITTEN AND ILLUSTRATED BY

DESIGNED BY JOE McGARRY

First published by Pitch Publishing, 2021

Pitch Publishing
A2 Yeoman Gate
Yeoman Way
Worthing
Sussex
BN13 3QZ
www.pitchpublishing.co.uk
info@pitchpublishing.co.uk

A CIP catalogue record is available for this book
from the British Library.

ISBN: 978 1 80150 018 0

Typesetting and origination by Pitch Publishing
Printed and bound in India by Replika Press Pvt. Ltd.

1001 TRIVIA QUESTIONS: MANCHESTER UNITED

Other books in this series:

1001 TRIVIA QUESTIONS: ARSENAL
1001 TRIVIA QUESTIONS: MANCHESTER CITY
1001 TRIVIA QUESTIONS: NEWCASTLE UNITED
1001 TRIVIA QUESTIONS: TOTTENHAM HOTSPUR
1001 TRIVIA QUESTIONS: WEST HAM UNITED
1001 TRIVIA QUESTIONS: THIS DAY IN WORLD FOOTBALL

ACKNOWLEDGEMENTS

Thanks to Joe McGarry for his brilliant design work and his technical expertise. There would be no books without him!

Thanks to Debs McGarry for the research and art assistance.

Thanks to Luke McGarry for picking up the slack on the other features while we worked on this.

Thanks to all three for their patience!

Additional thanks to Tom and Andy at "Shoot! The Breeze" podcast and Rob Stokes for the additional research and scans!

ABOUT STEVE McGARRY

A former record sleeve designer, whose clients included Joy Division, Steve McGarry is one of the most prolific and widely-published cartoonists and illustrators that Britain has ever produced. In the UK alone, his national newspaper daily strips include "Badlands", which ran for a dozen years in The Sun, "The Diary of Rock & Pop" in the Daily Star, "Pop Culture" in Today and "World Soccer Diary" in The Sun.

Over his four-decade career he has regularly graced the pages of soccer magazines Match, Match of the Day and Shoot! and his comics work ranges from Romeo in the 1970s and Look-In, Tiger and Oink! in the 1980s, SI for Kids and FHM in the 1990s, through to the likes of Viz, MAD and Toxic! When The People launched his Steve McGarry's 20th Century Heroes series, they billed him as the world's top cartoonist.

His sports features have been published worldwide since 1982 and he currently has two features – "Biographic" and "Kid Town" – in newspaper syndication, with a client list that includes the New York Daily News and The Washington Post.

In recent years, he has also created story art for such movies as "Despicable Me 2", "The Minions" and "The Secret Life of Pets".

Although Manchester born and bred, Steve has been based in California since 1989. A two-term former President of the National Cartoonists Society, his honours include Illustrator of the Year awards from the NCS and the Australian Cartoonists Association, and he is a recipient of the prestigious Silver T-Square for "outstanding service to the profession of cartooning". In 2013, he was elected President of the NCS Foundation, the charitable arm of the National Cartoonists Society. He is also the founder and director of US comics festival NCSFest.

1001 QUESTIONS

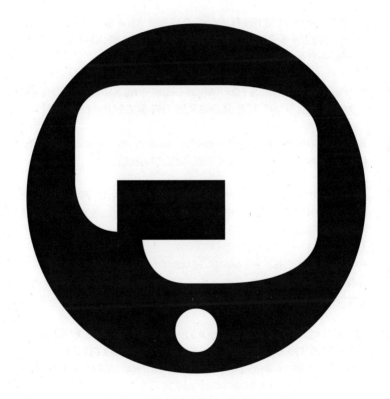

FERGIE TIME

THE LONGEST-SERVING MANAGER IN *MANCHESTER UNITED* HISTORY, *SIR ALEX FERGUSON'S* TROPHY HAUL AT THE CLUB INCLUDED 13 LEAGUE TITLES, FIVE FA CUPS, TWO UEFA CHAMPIONS LEAGUES AND THE UEFA CUP WINNERS' CUP. BORN IN GLASGOW IN 1941, EARLY IN HIS CAREER HE PLAYED PART-TIME WHILE WORKING IN THE GLASGOW SHIPYARDS. HE WAS KNIGHTED IN *THE QUEEN'S* 1991 BIRTHDAY HONOURS LIST.

1 HAVING LAUNCHED HIS PLAYING CAREER AS A 16-YEAR-OLD STRIKER WITH *QUEEN'S PARK*, HE WON A SCOTTISH SECOND DIVISION TITLE IN 1963 WITH WHICH CLUB?

2 IN 1966 HIS 31 GOALS FOR WHICH CLUB -- NICKNAMED *"THE PARS"* -- MADE HIM JOINT TOP SCORER IN THE SCOTTISH LEAGUE?

3 HIS £65,000 TRANSFER TO WHICH CLUB IN 1966 WAS A RECORD FEE FOR A TRANSFER BETWEEN TWO SCOTTISH CLUBS?

4 HE WON A SCOTTISH SECOND DIVISION TITLE WITH *FALKIRK* BEFORE ENDING HIS PLAYING DAYS AT WHICH CLUB KNOWN AS "*THE HONEST MEN*"?

5 HAVING LAUNCHED HIS MANAGEMENT CAREER WITH *EAST STIRLINGSHIRE*, HE WON A SCOTTISH DIVISION ONE TITLE WITH WHICH CLUB IN 1977 BEFORE BEING SACKED THE FOLLOWING YEAR?

6 HE WON MULTIPLE HONOURS AS MANAGER OF *ABERDEEN*, INCLUDING THREE LEAGUE TITLES AND THE 1983 EUROPEAN CUP WINNERS' CUP -- WHO DID THEY BEAT IN THAT EUROPEAN FINAL?

7 WITH THE DEATH OF *JOCK STEIN*, *FERGUSON* STEPPED UP TO MANAGE *SCOTLAND* AND STEER HIS COUNTRY TO THE 1986 WORLD CUP. THEY WERE ELIMINATED AT THE GROUP STAGE, LOSING TO *DENMARK* AND *WEST GERMANY* BUT GAINING A SINGLE POINT AGAINST WHICH NATION?

8 WHAT WAS THE FIRST TROPHY *FERGUSON* WON AS MANAGER OF *MANCHESTER UNITED*?

9   **FERGUSON'S** FINAL GAME IN CHARGE OF **UNITED** WAS A 5-5 DRAW AGAINST WHICH TEAM IN 2013?

10   ITEMS FROM HIS PERSONAL COLLECTION OF WHICH ITEM RAISED £2.2 MILLION AT AUCTION BY **CHRISTIE'S** IN 2014?

DORTMUNDERS

HAVING SCORED FIVE GOALS AND BEEN NAMED GOLDEN PLAYER AT THE 2017 UEFA EUROPEAN UNDER-17 CHAMPIONSHIP, *JADON SANCHO* LEFT *MANCHESTER CITY* FOR *BORUSSIA DORTMUND*. WITHIN WEEKS OF COMPLETING THE TRANSFER, HE WAS NAMED IN THE 2017 FIFA U-17 WORLD CUP SQUAD -- BUT *DORTMUND* INSISTED THAT HE BE WITHDRAWN AFTER THE OPENING ROUND OF GAMES. *ENGLAND* STORMED THROUGH THE TOURNAMENT AND THE ABSENT *SANCHO* WAS REWARDED WITH A WINNER'S MEDAL.

1 WHICH YOUNG *BELGIUM* INTERNATIONAL WAS LOANED OUT FROM *UNITED* TO *BORUSSIA DORTMUND* IN 2015?

2 *BORUSSIA DORTMUND* KNOCKED *UNITED* OUT IN THE SEMI-FINALS OF THE UEFA CHAMPIONS LEAGUE, WINNING BOTH LEGS 1-0 ON THE WAY TO TRIUMPHING IN THE 1997 FINAL. WHO WAS THE *BORUSSIA DORTMUND* MANAGER WHO WOULD LATER WIN A SECOND CHAMPIONS LEAGUE AS PART OF A HISTORIC TREBLE WITH *BAYERN MUNICH*?

3 NAME *ARMENIA'S* ALL-TIME TOP GOALSCORER, WHO JOINED *UNITED* FROM *DORTMUND* IN 2016 AND WAS A UEFA EUROPA LEAGUE WINNER THE FOLLOWING YEAR.

4 WHEN *UNITED* BECAME THE FIRST ENGLISH TEAM TO COMPETE IN THE EUROPEAN CUP IN THE 1956-57 SEASON, THEY DEFEATED *DORTMUND* 3-2 IN THE ROUND OF 16 TO ADVANCE TO THE QUARTER-FINALS, WHERE THEY BEAT *ATHLETIC BILBAO* 6-5 OVER TWO LEGS. WHICH TEAM ELIMINATED *UNITED* IN THE SEMI-FINALS?

5 NAME THE FIRST AMERICAN-BORN PLAYER TO SIGN FOR **UNITED**. HE LED RESERVE TEAM SCORING FOR THE REDS BUT WORK PERMIT PROBLEMS SAW HIM LEAVE FOR **DORTMUND** IN 1996, WHERE THE CALIFORNIAN BECAME THE FIRST AMERICAN TO WIN THE UEFA CHAMPIONS LEAGUE.

6 WHO WON TWO CONSECUTIVE LEAGUE TITLES WITH **DORTMUND** BEFORE WINNING THE PREMIER LEAGUE IN THE FIRST OF HIS THREE SEASON WITH **UNITED**, FOLLOWING WHICH HE RETURNED TO THE GERMAN CLUB IN 2014?

7 IN WHICH EUROPEAN COMPETITION DID **UNITED** BEAT **DORTMUND** 10-1 OVER TWO LEGS IN 1964, EN ROUTE TO A SEMI-FINAL LOSS TO EVENTUAL WINNERS **FERENCVÁROS**?

THE RELUCTANT HERO

JUST WEEKS AFTER SIGNING FOR *UNITED*, *HARRY GREGG* WAS THE HERO OF THE 1958 MUNICH AIR DISASTER THAT DECIMATED THE YOUNG TEAM. IGNORING HIS OWN INJURIES, *GREGG* RETURNED TWICE TO THE BURNING FUSELAGE TO PULL PASSENGERS FROM THE WRECKAGE, INCLUDING *VERENA LUKIC* AND HER BABY *VESNA*, AND HIS TEAMMATES *BOBBY CHARLTON* AND *DENNIS VIOLETT*. *GREGG* ALWAYS DOWNPLAYED HIS HEROISM -- BUT IN THE WORDS OF *GEORGE BEST*: "WHAT *HARRY* DID THAT NIGHT WAS ABOUT MORE THAN JUST BRAVERY. IT WAS ABOUT GOODNESS."

1 *GREGG* LEFT HIS NATIVE *NORTHERN IRELAND* TO SIGN FOR WHICH ENGLISH CLUB IN 1952?

2 THAT CLUB AND THE *NORTHERN IRELAND* TEAM WERE SIMULTANEOUSLY MANAGED BY WHICH LEGENDARY FORMER *MANCHESTER CITY* INSIDE-FORWARD?

3 *GREGG'S* £23,750 TRANSFER TO *UNITED* WAS A WORLD RECORD FEE FOR A GOALKEEPER -- WHO DID HE REPLACE AS *UNITED'S* FIRST CHOICE GOALKEEPER?

4 *GREGG* KEPT GOAL IN *UNITED'S* 1958 FA CUP FINAL LOSS TO WHICH TEAM?

5 HE PLAYED FOR **NORTHERN IRELAND** AT THE 1958 WORLD CUP, WHERE HE WAS VOTED BEST GOALKEEPER AND WAS NAMED IN THE TOURNAMENT'S ALL-STAR TEAM. WHICH **UNITED** PLAYER REPRESENTED **ENGLAND** IN THE TOURNAMENT?

6 GREGG HAD A BRIEF SPELL PLAYING FOR WHICH CLUB AFTER LEAVING **UNITED** IN DECEMBER, 1966?

7 HE SUCCEEDED **ARTHUR ROWLEY** AS MANAGER OF WHICH TEAM IN 1968, A CLUB WHOSE SUBSEQUENT MANAGERS INCLUDE **ASA HARTFORD, JOHN BOND, KEVIN RATCLIFFE, GRAHAM TURNER** AND **STEVE COTTERILL**.

8 HIS SECOND MANAGEMENT POST WAS WITH WHICH CLUB, SUBSEQUENTLY MANAGED BY **JOHN TOSHACK, BRENDAN ROGERS, ROBERTO MARTINEZ** AND **PAULO SOUSA**?

9 **HARRY** SPENT THREE YEARS IN CHARGE OF WHICH CLUB, WHOSE LONGEST-SERVING MANAGER WOULD LATER BE **DARIO GRADI**?

10 HE WAS ASSISTANT MANAGER TO WHICH FORMER **UNITED** PLAYER AT **SWINDON TOWN**, THE DISCORD BETWEEN THE PAIR SO BAD THAT THEY WERE BOTH SACKED IN 1985?

11 IN HIS FINAL MANAGEMENT JOB, **HARRY GREGG** WAS ASSISTANT TO **BOB STOKOE** AT WHICH CLUB BEFORE TAKING THE REINS WHEN **STOKOE** LEFT IN 1986?

PORTUGUESE IMPORTS

HAVING PLAYED MOST OF HIS YOUTH FOOTBALL IN HIS NATIVE PORTUGAL WITH **BOAVISTA, BRUNO FERNANDES** LAUNCHED HIS SENIOR CAREER IN ITALY. A SEASON IN THE SECOND TIER WITH **NOVARA** WAS FOLLOWED BY MOVES TO SERIE A SIDES **UDINESE** AND **SAMPDORIA**. HE RETURNED TO PORTUGAL IN 2017 TO WIN MULTIPLE CUP HONOURS WITH **SPORTING CP**. TWICE PRIMEIRA LIGA PLAYER OF THE YEAR, HE JOINED **UNITED** IN 2020 IN A £47 MILLION DEAL WITH A POTENTIAL £21 MILLION IN ADD-ONS.

FROM WHICH PORTUGUESE
CLUB DID **UNITED** SIGN:

1   **NANI** (2007)

2   **VICTOR LINDELÖF** (2017)

3   **CRISTIANO RONALDO** (2003)

4   **ANDERSON** (2007)

5   **DIOGO DALOT** (2018)

6   **MARCOS ROJO** (2014)

7   **BEBÉ** (2010)

8   **ALEX TELLES** (2020)

CHARITY CASES

UNITED HOLD THE RECORD OF 30 APPEARANCES IN THE FA COMMUNITY SHIELD, FORMERLY THE FA CHARITY SHIELD. THE TRADITIONAL SEASON OPENER PITS THE REIGNING CHAMPIONS AGAINST THE FA CUP WINNERS, ALTHOUGH THAT HAS VARIED ON OCCASION WHEN A CLUB HAD PRIOR COMMITMENTS, OR WAS A LEAGUE AND FA CUP DOUBLE-WINNER, AND A REPLACEMENT TEAM WAS DRAFTED IN. THE TROPHY IS SHARED IN THE EVENT OF A DRAW. **UNITED** HAVE WON THE TROPHY OUTRIGHT 17 TIMES, AND SHARED IT A FURTHER FOUR TIMES, FOR A TOTAL OF 21 WINS.

SEE HOW MANY OF THOSE 21 OPPONENTS YOU CAN NAME:

1   1908: SOUTHERN FOOTBALL LEAGUE WINNERS

2   1911: SOUTHERN FOOTBALL LEAGUE WINNERS

3   1952: FA CUP WINNERS

4   1956: FA CUP WINNERS

5   1957: FA CUP WINNERS

6   1965: FA CUP WINNERS

7   1967: FA CUP WINNERS

8   1977: FIRST DIVISION WINNERS

9   1983: FIRST DIVISION WINNERS

10   1990: FIRST DIVISION WINNERS

11   1993: FA CUP WINNERS

12   1994: PREMIER LEAGUE RUNNERS-UP

13   1996: PREMIER LEAGUE RUNNERS-UP

14   1997: FA CUP WINNERS

NERAZZURRI!

HAVING WON MULTIPLE HONOURS WITH *UNITED*, INCLUDING TWO PREMIER LEAGUE TITLES AND THE EUROPEAN CUP WINNERS' CUP, *PAUL INCE* JOINED *INTERNAZIONALE* IN A £7.5 MILLION TRANSFER IN THE SUMMER OF 1995. HE SPENT TWO SEASONS WITH THE *"NERAZZURRI"* BEFORE RETURNING TO BRITISH FOOTBALL TO ENABLE HIS SON, *TOM*, TO ATTEND SCHOOL IN ENGLAND.

1 WHICH *FRANCE* INTERNATIONAL FULL-BACK JOINED *UNITED* FROM *INTERNAZIONALE* IN 1999, GOING ON TO WIN FIVE PREMIER LEAGUE TITLES, THE UEFA CHAMPIONS LEAGUE AND MORE? HE SUBSEQUENTLY HAD TWO SEASONS AT *ARSENAL*.

2 AN *ENGLAND* INTERNATIONAL WHO WON EVERY DOMESTIC HONOUR AND THE EUROPA CUP WITH *UNITED*, WHICH WINGER TURNED ATTACKING FULL-BACK LEFT THE REDS FOR *INTERNAZIONALE* IN 2020 AND WON A SERIE A TITLE BEFORE JOINING *ASTON VILLA*?

3 *UNITED* BEAT *INTERNAZIONALE* 3-1 ON AGGREGATE ON THE WAY TO THE 1999 UEFA CHAMPIONS LEAGUE FINAL VICTORY OVER *BAYERN MUNICH*. NAME ANOTHER TEAM *UNITED* FACED EN ROUTE TO BECOMING EUROPEAN CHAMPIONS THAT SEASON.

4 HAVING WON HONOURS WITH *COLO-COLO*, *RIVER PLATE*, *BARCELONA* AND *ARSENAL*, WHICH FORWARD LEFT *UNITED* FOR *INTERNAZIONALE* IN 2019 AND WON A SERIE A TITLE?

5 NAME THE ARGENTINE WHO WON HONOURS WITH *ESTUDIANTES*, *PARMA*, *LAZIO* AND *INTERNAZIONALE* AND LEFT *UNITED* FOR *CHELSEA* AFTER WINNING THE PREMIER LEAGUE IN 2003.

6 WHO IS THE ONLY MAN TO MANAGE BOTH *MANCHESTER UNITED* AND *INTERNAZIONALE*?

7 WHICH STRIKER WON HONOURS WITH *ANDERLECHT*, PLAYED IN THE PREMIER LEAGUE FOR *CHELSEA*, *WEST BROMWICH ALBION*, *EVERTON* AND *UNITED* BEFORE WINNING A SERIE A TITLE WITH *INTERNAZIONALE*?

8 WHICH SERBIAN DEFENDER, A UEFA CHAMPIONS LEAGUE AND QUINTUPLE PREMIER LEAGUE WINNER WITH *UNITED*, RETIRED AFTER TWO SEASONS WITH *INTERNAZIONALE* FROM 2014 TO 2016?

9 WHICH *URUGUAY* STRIKER WON THE PREMIER LEAGUE AND FA CUP WITH *UNITED* AND THE UEFA EUROPA LEAGUE WITH *ATLÉTICO MADRID* BEFORE JOINING *INTERNAZIONALE* IN 2011?

10 WHICH 1998 WORLD CUP AND EURO 2000 WINNER JOINED *UNITED* FROM *INTERNAZIONALE* TO REPLACE *JAAP STAM*?

CALEDONIAN KING

THE ONLY SCOTTISH FOOTBALLER TO WIN THE BALLON D'OR, *DENIS LAW* SPENT 11 SEASONS WITH *UNITED*, SCORING 237 GOALS IN 404 GAMES.

LAW WAS INDUCTED IN THE *SCOTTISH FOOTBALL HALL OF FAME* IN ITS INAUGURAL YEAR OF 2004. NAME THESE OTHER *UNITED* INDUCTEES:

1 2004: FORMER *MANCHESTER CITY* AND *LIVERPOOL* PLAYER WHO WAS PORTRAYED BY ACTOR *DOUGRAY SCOTT* IN THE 2011 TELEVISION DRAMA *"UNITED"*.

2 2004: HIS SON HAD THREE TERMS AS *PETERBOROUGH UNITED* MANAGER, EARNING THE CLUB MULTIPLE PROMOTIONS.

3 2005: DURING HIS PLAYING DAYS, HE WAS THE FOCUS OF AN AD CAMPAIGN FOR A BEER THAT *"REFRESHES THE PARTS OTHER BEERS CANNOT REACH"*.

4 2006: INDUCTED IN THE SAME YEAR AS *BRIAN LAUDRUP*, MAKING THEM THE FIRST PLAYERS FROM OUTSIDE OF SCOTLAND TO BE HONOURED, HE WAS A MEMBER OF THE *SWEDEN* TEAM THAT FINISHED IN THIRD PLACE IN THE 1994 WORLD CUP.

5 2007: HE PLAYED IN TWO WORLD CUPS FOR *SCOTLAND* AND LATER MANAGED THE NATIONAL TEAM.

6 2008: CAPPED 91 TIMES BY *SCOTLAND*, HE WAS AN FA CUP WINNER WITH *UNITED* IN 1990 AND WON MULTIPLE HONOURS IN HIS TWO SPELLS WITH *ABERDEEN*, INCLUDING THE 1983 EUROPEAN CUP WINNERS' CUP.

7 2009: WINGER WHO WON THE SCOTTISH CUP WITH *CELTIC* IN 1937, THE ENGLISH FA CUP WITH *UNITED* IN 1948, AND THE IRISH CUP WITH *DERRY CITY* IN 1954.

8 2010: VOTED THE GREATEST GOALKEEPER IN *RANGERS'* HISTORY, WITH WHOM HE WON FIVE LEAGUE TITLES, A FORMER *OLDHAM ATHLETIC* STALWART WHO PLAYED TWO GAMES ON LOAN WITH *UNITED* IN THE 2001 TITLE RUN-IN.

9 2011: A 1968 EUROPEAN CUP WINNER WITH *UNITED*, FOR WHOM HE PLAYED 401 GAMES, HE WAS APPOINTED ASSISTANT MANAGER IN 1972 AFTER RETIRING.

10 2012: HE WON THE LEAGUE WITH *LEEDS UNITED* AND THE 1983 FA CUP WITH *UNITED*, HIS DAUGHTER HAS ENJOYED A SUCCESSFUL CAREER IN TV SPORTS BROADCASTING.

11 2013: THE CLUB'S RECORD SIGNING WHEN RECRUITED BY *FRANK O'FARRELL* FROM *ABERDEEN* IN 1972 FOR £120,000.

12 2013: *SCOTLAND* INTERNATIONAL WHO WAS SUCCEEDED AS MANAGER OF *CHELSEA* BY *DAVE SEXTON* -- AND THEN AGAIN AS MANAGER OF *MANCHESTER UNITED!*

13 2015: HE SPENT TWO SEASONS PLAYING FOR *UNITED* -- DURING WHICH TIME THE CLUB WERE RELEGATED -- BUT AMONG HIS MANY HONOURS WERE LEAGUE TITLES WON AS BOTH A PLAYER AND SUBSEQUENT MANAGER OF *ARSENAL.*

THE PINT-SIZED TERRIER

DIMINUTIVE AND BALDING, **NOBBY STILES** WORE DENTURES AND CONTACT LENSES WHEN HE PLAYED -- BUT THE PINT-SIZED TERRIER POLICED THE MIDFIELD FOR CLUB AND COUNTRY AND WON THE GAME'S HIGHEST HONOURS. BORN IN THE CELLAR OF HIS FAMILY HOME IN MANCHESTER, DURING A WAR-TIME AIR RAID, ON MAY 18, 1942, THE SON OF A FUNERAL DIRECTOR, HE SPENT 11 YEARS WITH **UNITED**, WINNING TWO LEAGUE TITLES AND THE EUROPEAN CUP, AND WAS A WORLD CUP WINNER WITH **ENGLAND** IN 1966.

1   **NOBBY STILES** AND **BOBBY CHARLTON** ARE TWO OF THE ONLY THREE ENGLISHMEN TO WIN THE EUROPEAN CUP AND THE WORLD CUP -- WHICH **LIVERPOOL** PLAYER IS THE THIRD?

2   **STILES** AND **CHARLTON** WERE TWO OF THE **ENGLAND** INTERNATIONALS IN THE **UNITED** TEAM THAT WON THE EUROPEAN CUP IN 1968 -- HOW MANY OTHERS CAN YOU NAME?

3   EXCLUDING ANY CARETAKERS, WHO WAS THE ONLY OTHER **UNITED** MANAGER UNDER WHOM **NOBBY STILES** PLAYED OTHER THAN **SIR MATT BUSBY**?

4   **STILES** JOINED WHICH CLUB IN 1971?

5   **STILES** PLAYED UNDER WHICH FORMER TEAMMATE AT **PRESTON NORTH END**, BECOMING CARETAKER-MANAGER WHEN THAT INCUMBENT RESIGNED?

6   IN 1977, **STILES** RETURNED TO **PRESTON** TO REPLACE WHICH FORMER MANAGER OF **SHEFFIELD WEDNESDAY** AND **EVERTON**?

7   IN THE EARLY 1980S, HE HEADED ACROSS THE ATLANTIC TO MANAGE WHICH NASL SIDE, WHERE HIS ROSTER INCLUDED **PETER LORIMER** AND **PETER BEARDSLEY**?

8   **NOBBY'S** FINAL SPELL IN MANAGEMENT CAME WITH HIS BRIEF TENURE OF WHICH MIDLANDS CLUB IN 1985-86?

9   IN 2000, FOLLOWING A MEDIA CAMPAIGN, *NOBBY* WAS ONE OF FIVE MEMBERS OF THE 1966 *ENGLAND* WORLD CUP TEAM WHO FINALLY RECEIVED OFFICIAL HONOURS RECOGNITION, HAVING BEEN PREVIOUSLY OVERLOOKED. HE WAS AWARDED THE MBE -- AS WERE WHICH FOUR OTHER PLAYERS?

10   IN WHICH YEAR DID *NOBBY STILES* PASS AWAY?

THE DUTCH MASTER

ARNOLD MÜHREN JOINED **UNITED** IN 1982 HAVING WON THE 1973 EUROPEAN CUP WITH **AJAX** AND THE UEFA CUP IN 1981 WITH **IPSWICH TOWN**. HE WON THE FA CUP WITH **UNITED** IN HIS DEBUT SEASON BUT AFTER BEING OMITTED FROM THE SQUAD THAT WON THE FA CUP IN 1985, RETURNED TO **AJAX**. HIS SECOND SPELL IN AMSTERDAM SAW HIM BECOME ONE OF THE RARE BREED OF PLAYERS TO WIN ALL THREE MAJOR UEFA-ORGANISED CLUB COMPETITIONS, WHEN HE ADDED THE 1987 EUROPEAN CUP WINNERS' CUP TO HIS TROPHY HAUL. THE FOLLOWING YEAR, HE HELPED THE **NETHERLANDS** WIN THE EUROPEAN CHAMPIONSHIP.

NAME THESE PLAYERS WHO WON THE EUROPEAN CUP/UEFA CHAMPIONS LEAGUE WITH A TEAM OTHER THAN **UNITED**:

1 TWO PLAYERS WHO WERE IN THE **NOTTINGHAM FOREST** TEAMS THAT WON THE EUROPEAN CUP IN 1979 AND 1980.

2 IN 2012, A UEFA CHAMPIONS LEAGUE WINNER WITH HIS CLUB AND A UEFA EUROPEAN CHAMPIONSHIP WINNER WITH HIS COUNTRY.

3 SOUTH AMERICAN WHO WON WITH **REAL MADRID** IN 2014.

4 WORLD CUP-WINNING GOALKEEPER WHO WON IN 1993.

5 A NON-PLAYING MEDAL WINNER IN 1968 WHO WON HIS SECOND CHAMPIONS LEAGUE WHILE WITH **ASTON VILLA**.

6 TWO YEARS BEFORE SIGNING FOR **UNITED** HE GAINED A WINNER'S MEDAL IN A 2-1 WIN OVER **BORUSSIA DORTMUND** AT **WEMBLEY**.

7 13 YEARS AFTER WINNING WITH **AJAX**, HE GAINED HIS SECOND MEDAL WITH HIS 2008 PENALTY SHOOT-OUT HEROICS AGAINST **CHELSEA**.

8 WINNER IN 2001 AND 2008 -- THE FIRST **ENGLAND** PLAYER TO WIN TWO CHAMPIONS LEAGUES WITH TWO DIFFERENT TEAMS

9 FIVE-TIMES CHAMPIONS LEAGUE WINNER, THE FIRST-EVER PLAYER TO SCORE IN TWO FINALS FOR TWO DIFFERENT WINNING TEAMS.

10 A SQUAD MEMBER WITH *UNITED* IN 2008 AND A TRIPLE WINNER WITH *BARCELONA*.

11 A THREE-TIMES WINNER WITH *BARCELONA*, FOLLOWING WHICH HE PLAYED FOR *UNITED* AND *MIDDLESBROUGH*.

12 *SWEDEN* INTERNATIONAL WHO WON A CHAMPIONS LEAGUE MEDAL IN 2006.

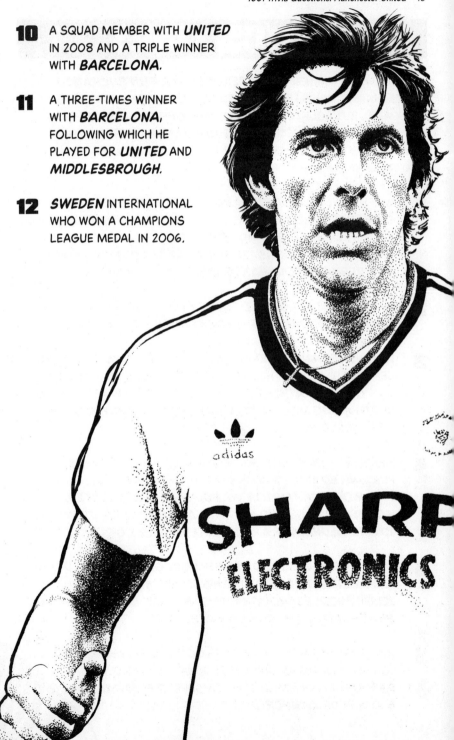

LATICS LINKS

A SCOTTISH CUP WINNER WITH **ABERDEEN**, **MARTIN BUCHAN** JOINED **UNITED** IN 1972. IN HIS FIRST SEASON AS CLUB CAPTAIN, UNITED WERE RELEGATED, BUT BOUNCED BACK AS CHAMPIONS AND WENT ON TO WIN THE 1977 FA CUP. THAT VICTORY MADE **BUCHAN** THE FIRST PLAYER TO CAPTAIN BOTH SCOTTISH AND FA CUP-WINNING TEAMS. HE ENDED HIS PLAYING CAREER WITH TWO SEASONS AT **OLDHAM ATHLETIC**.

1 WHICH **REPUBLIC OF IRELAND** INTERNATIONAL FULL-BACK JOINED **UNITED** FROM **OLDHAM ATHLETIC** IN 1990 AND WENT ON TO WIN SEVEN PREMIER LEAGUE TITLES, THE UEFA CHAMPIONS LEAGUE, THE EUROPEAN CUP WINNERS' CUP AND MORE BEFORE MOVING ON TO **WOLVERHAMPTON WANDERERS** AFTER 12 SEASONS?

2 WHICH LEGENDARY **UNITED** PLAYER SPENT JUST SEVEN GAMES IN CHARGE OF **OLDHAM ATHLETIC** IN 2019 BEFORE RESIGNING?

3 WHICH **ENGLAND** INTERNATIONAL CENTRE-HALF, WHO WON TWO LEAGUE TITLES AND THE FA CUP WITH **UNITED**, LEFT IN 1913 TO JOIN **OLDHAM ATHLETIC** IN A RECORD £1,500 TRANSFER, LATER RETURNING TO MANAGE **"THE LATICS"** AFTER THE END OF THE FIRST WORLD WAR?

4 WHICH LEFT-BACK MADE TEN PREMIER LEAGUE APPEARANCES FOR **UNITED** IN THE 2015-16 SEASON, HAD LOAN SPELLS WITH **WOLVERHAMPTON WANDERERS**, **LEEDS UNITED**, **SCUNTHORPE UNITED** AND **TRANMERE ROVERS** BEFORE JOINING **OLDHAM** ON A PERMANENT DEAL IN 2020?

5 WHICH GOALKEEPER, WHO WAS SENT OUT ON LOAN TO **OLDHAM** AND **AIRDRIEONIANS** DURING HIS DECADE WITH **UNITED**, JOINED **MIDDLESBROUGH** IN 1995 AND WENT ON TO PLAY FOR **BRADFORD CITY** AND **WIGAN ATHLETIC**?

6 WHICH WELL-TRAVELLED SCOTTISH GOALKEEPER, WHO PLAYED FOR BOTH **OLDHAM** AND **UNITED**, WAS REPORTEDLY DIAGNOSED WITH A MILD FORM OF SCHIZOPHRENIA WHILE PLAYING FOR **RANGERS**?

7   WHICH **UNITED** AND **ENGLAND** GOALSCORING GREAT, WHO SCORED TWICE IN THE 1948 FA CUP FINAL WIN, HAD TWO SPELLS AS **OLDHAM ATHLETIC** MANAGER?

8   BORN IN 1947, WHICH **UNITED** DEFENDER FELL OUT OF FAVOUR UNDER **FRANK O'FARRELL** AND JOINED **OLDHAM** IN 1972? HE HELPED **"THE LATICS"** WIN PROMOTION IN 1974 AND LATER BRIEFLY PLAYED FOR **STOCKPORT COUNTY**.

9   WHICH TEENAGER, DESPITE SCORING HAT-TRICKS FOR **UNITED** AGAINST **LEEDS UNITED** AND **TOTTENHAM HOTSPUR**, WAS SOLD TO **BRIGHTON & HOVE ALBION** IN 1980, THEN MOVED ON TO **LEEDS UNITED**, BEFORE BECOMING A CLUB LEGEND IN HIS EIGHT SUCCESSFUL YEARS WITH **OLDHAM**? HE LATER RETURNED TO MANAGE THE CLUB.

10   WHICH YORKSHIREMAN WAS **UNITED'S** RECORD SIGNING IN 1958, LATER PLAYING FOR **OLDHAM** AND **STOCKPORT COUNTY**?

FERGIE'S FLEDGLINGS

IN 2014, **SALFORD CITY** WERE TAKEN OVER BY FORMER **UNITED** PLAYERS **NICKY BUTT, RYAN GIGGS, GARY NEVILLE, PHIL NEVILLE** AND **PAUL SCHOLES,** EACH OWNING 10% OF THE CLUB, WITH SINGAPOREAN BUSINESSMAN **PETER LIM** OWNING THE REST. **DAVID BECKHAM** PURCHASED A 10% SHARE FROM **LIM** IN 2019. ALL SIX PLAYERS WERE PART OF THE GROUP DUBBED **"THE CLASS OF '92"** -- YOUNGSTERS WHO EMERGED THROUGH THE YOUTH RANKS TO TAKE **UNITED** TO NEW HEIGHTS. THE LARGER GROUP OF YOUNG PLAYERS TO MAKE THEIR WAY TO THE TOP DURING **SIR ALEX FERGUSON'S** TENURE WAS NICKNAMED **"FERGIE'S FLEDGLINGS"** -- IDENTIFY THE FOLLOWING:

1 A LEAGUE CUP WINNER WITH **LEICESTER CITY** AS A PLAYER AND A MANAGER THAT BROUGHT SUCCESS TO **COVENTRY CITY,** THE GOAL HE SCORED AGAINST **NOTTINGHAM FOREST** THAT SPARKED **UNITED'S** SUCCESSFUL 1990 FA CUP CAMPAIGN IS SAID TO HAVE KEPT UNDER-PRESSURE **ALEX FERGUSON** IN THE MANAGER'S JOB.

2 **ENGLAND** CENTRE-HALF WHO WON MULTIPLE HONOURS WITH THE REDS -- INCLUDING FIVE PREMIER LEAGUE TITLES AND TWO UEFA CHAMPIONS LEAGUES -- BEFORE JOINING **SUNDERLAND** IN 2011.

3 **NORTHERN IRELAND** INTERNATIONAL WINGER WHO WON THE FA YOUTH CUP WITH **UNITED** AND THE LEAGUE CUP WITH **BLACKBURN ROVERS** IN A CAREER THAT TOOK HIM TO **NEWCASTLE UNITED, WIGAN ATHLETIC, SHEFFIELD UNITED** AND MORE.

4 **SCOTLAND** INTERNATIONAL WHO, DESPITE HAVING HIS CAREER DISRUPTED BY A LENGTHY BATTLE WITH ULCERATIVE COLITIS, WON FIVE PREMIER LEAGUE TITLES, A UEFA CHAMPIONS LEAGUE AND MORE DURING HIS 20 YEARS WITH **UNITED.**

5 **ENGLAND** MIDFIELDER WHO PLAYED FOR **GREAT BRITAIN** AT THE 2012 OLYMPICS, WON THE PREMIER LEAGUE IN 2013 WITH **UNITED,** WON PROMOTION WITH **LEICESTER CITY,** PLAYED IN FA CUP FINALS WITH **ASTON VILLA** AND **WATFORD** AND SPENT TWO SEASONS WITH **EVERTON.**

6   *REPUBLIC OF IRELAND* CENTRAL DEFENDER WHO WON MULTIPLE HONOURS WITH *UNITED*, SPENT SEVEN SEASONS AT *SUNDERLAND* AND ENDED HIS PLAYING DAYS WITH *READING*.

7   *ENGLAND* STRIKER WHOSE HONOURS INCLUDE A PREMIER LEAGUE WITH *UNITED*, THE FA CUP WITH *ARSENAL*, AND WHO PLAYED A SEASON WITH *WATFORD* BEFORE JOINING *BRIGHTON & HOVE ALBION* IN 2020.

8   *NORTHERN IRELAND* CENTRAL DEFENDER WHO WON MULTIPLE HONOURS WITH *UNITED*, SPENT THREE SEASONS AT *WEST BROMWICH ALBION* AND THEN WON THE FA CUP WITH *LEICESTER CITY* IN 2021.

HARRY'S GAME

HARRY MAGUIRE FOLLOWED HIS QUARTER-FINAL GOAL AGAINST **SWEDEN** IN THE 2018 WORLD CUP WITH A QUARTER-FINAL GOAL AGAINST **UKRAINE** AT EURO 2020. THE FIRST **UNITED** PLAYER TO SCORE IN A EUROPEAN CHAMPIONSHIP TOURNAMENT WAS **BOBBY CHARLTON** IN 1962, BACK IN **ENGLAND'S** FIRST PARTICIPATION IN THE COMPETITION.

IDENTIFY THESE EURO GOALSCORERS WITH **UNITED** CONNECTIONS:

1   1980: IN ENGLAND'S FIRST TOURNAMENT IN A DECADE, WHICH TWO-TIME **CHELSEA** PLAYER OF THE YEAR, WHO HAD JOINED **UNITED** THE PREVIOUS YEAR, SCORED IN THE 1-1 DRAW WITH **BELGIUM**?

2   WHICH SUBSEQUENT **UNITED** PLAYER SCORED FOR **FRANCE** AT THE 1996 AND 2000 EUROPEAN CHAMPIONSHIPS?

3   NAME THE **TOTTENHAM HOTSPUR** FORWARD, WHO WOULD JOIN **UNITED** THE FOLLOWING YEAR AND GO ON TO UEFA CHAMPIONS LEAGUE GLORY, WHO SCORED TWICE FOR **ENGLAND** AT EURO 96?

4   WHICH TWO PLAYERS SCORED FOUR GOALS EACH IN 2004?

5   IN THE 2016 TOURNAMENT, WHICH TWO FORMER **UNITED** PLAYERS SCORED THREE GOALS EACH TO HELP THE EVENTUAL CHAMPIONS?

6   WHICH FORMER **UNITED** PLAYER SCORED TWICE AT EURO 2016 AND FOUR TIMES AT EURO 2020?

7   WHICH FORMER **UNITED** PLAYER SCORED TWICE FOR **NETHERLANDS** AT EURO 2020?

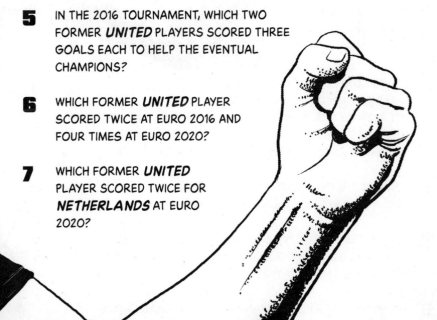

POTY POTPOURRI

SIGNED FROM **SPARTAK MOSCOW** IN 2006, **NEMANJA VIDIĆ** WAS THE LYNCHPIN OF THE **UNITED** DEFENCE FOR NINE SEASONS, WINNING A HOST OF HONOURS, INCLUDING FIVE PREMIER LEAGUE TITLES AND THE UEFA CHAMPIONS LEAGUE. CAPPED 56 TIMES BY **SERBIA**, HE WAS TWICE NAMED SERBIAN FOOTBALLER OF THE YEAR AND WON THE SERBIAN OVERSEAS PLAYER OF THE YEAR AWARD FOUR TIMES.

IDENTIFY THESE RECIPIENTS OF VARIOUS ANNUAL POTY AWARDS:

1 NAME THE THREE **UNITED** PLAYERS WHO HAVE WON THE DUTCH FOOTBALLER OF THE YEAR AWARD, WHICH SINCE 2006 HAS BEEN MERGED WITH THE GOUDEN SCHOEN (GOLDEN BOOT).

2 WHICH **UNITED** PLAYER WAS VOTED FOOTBALLER OF THE YEAR IN GERMANY IN 2013?

3 WHICH **UNITED** PLAYER, WINNER OF MULTIPLE ARMENIAN PLAYER OF THE YEAR AWARDS, WAS THE FIRST ARMENIAN TO BE NAMED CIS FOOTBALLER OF THE YEAR, THE FIRST PLAYER FROM POST-SOVIET COUNTRIES TO EARN THE AWARD?

4 WHO IS THE ONLY **UNITED** PLAYER NAMED FRENCH PLAYER OF THE YEAR?

5 NAME THE THREE **UNITED** PLAYERS WHO HAVE WON THE GULDBOLLEN, THE AWARD GIVEN TO THE SWEDISH FOOTBALLER OF THE YEAR.

6 WHICH **UNITED** PLAYER HAS WON FOOTBALLER OF THE YEAR AWARDS IN PORTUGAL, ENGLAND, SPAIN AND ITALY?

7 WHO ARE THE
THREE *UNITED*
PLAYERS
WHO WON
ARGENTINIAN
FOOTBALLER
OF THE YEAR
AWARDS?

8 WHO WAS NAMED
2010 KOREAN
FOOTBALLER OF
THE YEAR?

DEADLY DIMITAR

SEVEN TIMES BULGARIAN FOOTBALLER OF THE YEAR, *DIMITAR BERBATOV* WAS CAPPED 78 TIMES BY *BULGARIA* AND IS HIS COUNTRY'S ALL-TIME LEADING GOALSCORER. HE WON TWO PREMIER LEAGUE TITLES WITH *UNITED* AND THE 2010-11 PREMIER LEAGUE GOLDEN BOOT.

1 HAVING WON THE BULGARIAN CUP WITH *CSKA SOFIA*, *BERBATOV* JOINED WHICH BUNDESLIGA TEAM IN 2001?

2 HE WON THE 2008 LEAGUE CUP WITH WHICH ENGLISH TEAM?

3 HIS SEVENTH BULGARIAN FOOTBALLER OF THE YEAR AWARD ECLIPSED THE RECORD SET BY WHICH *BULGARIA* GREAT?

4 HE SHARED THE 2011 PREMIER LEAGUE GOLDEN BOOT WITH WHICH *MANCHESTER CITY* PLAYER?

5 HE LEFT *UNITED* IN 2012 FOR WHICH CLUB?

6 HE SIGNED FOR WHICH FRENCH SIDE IN 2014 AS A REPLACEMENT FOR THE INJURED *RADAMEL FALCAO*?

7 HE SPENT A SEASON WITH WHICH GREEK TEAM?

8 HE ENDED HIS PLAYING DAYS IN WHICH COUNTRY:
A) INDIA   B) THAILAND   C) JAPAN   D) CHINA

WORLD CUP WINNERS

ONE OF THE MOST DECORATED DEFENDERS IN SPANISH FOOTBALL HISTORY, **GERARD PIQUÉ** LAUNCHED HIS PROFESSIONAL CAREER WITH **UNITED**. A PRODUCT OF **BARCELONA'S** FAMED **"LA MASIA"** YOUTH PROGRAMME, HE MADE HIS **UNITED** DEBUT AT THE AGE OF 17. HE SPENT FOUR YEARS AT OLD TRAFFORD BEFORE RETURNING TO **BARCELONA** IN 2008.

PIQUÉ WON THE WORLD CUP WITH SPAIN IN 2010. IDENTIFY THESE OTHER WORLD CUP WINNERS WHO HAVE PLAYED FOR **UNITED:**

1 1966: THREE PLAYERS

2 1998: TWO PLAYERS

3 2002: ONE PLAYER

4 2010: **PIQUÉ** AND TWO OTHER PLAYERS

5 2014: ONE PLAYER

6 2018: ONE PLAYER

MANAGER MACARI

AFTER WINNING FOUR LEAGUE TITLES WITH **CELTIC** -- INCLUDING TWO LEAGUE AND SCOTTISH DOUBLES -- **SCOTLAND** INTERNATIONAL **LOU MACARI** JOINED **UNITED** IN 1973. FOLLOWING RELEGATION IN 1974, HE HELPED THE REDS RETURN TO THE TOP FLIGHT, AND WAS A MEMBER OF THE SIDE THAT WON THE FA CUP IN 1977, THE ONLY WIN IN THE FOUR FINALS HE REACHED DURING HIS 12 SEASONS AT **OLD TRAFFORD**. HE ENDING HIS PLAYING DAYS AND EMBARKED ON HIS MANAGEMENT CAREER AT **SWINDON TOWN**, GUIDING THE CLUB TO CONSECUTIVE PROMOTIONS. HE MANAGED **WEST HAM UNITED**, **CELTIC** AND **HUDDERSFIELD TOWN**, GUIDED **BIRMINGHAM CITY** TO THE FOOTBALL LEAGUE TROPHY AND STEERED **STOKE CITY** TO THE FOOTBALL LEAGUE TROPHY AND THE SECOND DIVISION TITLE IN THE FIRST OF TWO SPELLS WITH THE CLUB.

IDENTIFY THESE **UNITED** PLAYERS BY THE TEAMS THEY LATER MANAGED:

1 MIDDLESBROUGH, BRADFORD CITY, WEST BROMWICH ALBION, SHEFFIELD UNITED, THAILAND

2 COVENTRY CITY, PETERBOROUGH UNITED, NEW ENGLAND TEA MEN, JACKSONVILLE TEA MEN

3 MACCLESFIELD TOWN, MILTON KEYNES DONS, BLACKBURN ROVERS, NOTTS COUNTY, BLACKPOOL

4 NORTHWICH VICTORIA, MACCLESFIELD TOWN, NORTHERN IRELAND, STOCKPORT COUNTY, MORECAMBE

5 WALES, BLACKBURN ROVERS, MANCHESTER CITY, FULHAM, QUEENS PARK RANGERS, STOKE CITY, SOUTHAMPTON

6 COVENTRY CITY, SOUTHAMPTON, CELTIC, MIDDLESBROUGH, SCOTLAND

7 MILLWALL, ARSENAL, LEEDS UNITED, TOTTENHAM HOTSPUR

8 REPUBLIC OF IRELAND, WEST BROMWICH ALBION, SHAMROCK ROVERS, VANCOUVER WHITECAPS

9 *BRISTOL CITY, HEART OF MIDLOTHIAN, STOKE CITY*

10 *SHEFFIELD UNITED, HUDDERSFIELD TOWN, WIGAN ATHLETIC, CRYSTAL PALACE, BIRMINGHAM CITY, SUNDERLAND, HULL CITY, ASTON VILLA, SHEFFIELD WEDNESDAY, NEWCASTLE UNITED*

THE GREAT DIVIDE

IN A SCANDAL THAT ROCKED THE FOOTBALL WORLD IN THE EARLY 1900S, **MANCHESTER CITY** CAPTAIN **BILLY MEREDITH** WAS SUSPENDED FOR A YEAR WHEN IT EMERGED THAT HE HAD ATTEMPTED TO BRIBE **ASTON VILLA** PLAYERS TO THROW A CRUCIAL GAME. **CITY** WERE FINED £900 AND A NUMBER OF PLAYERS, DIRECTORS AND STAFF WERE ALSO SUSPENDED. **UNITED** STEPPED IN TO SIGN **MEREDITH** WHILE HE WAS STILL ON SUSPENSION, AND IN JANUARY OF 1907, SEVEN MONTHS AFTER PUTTING PEN TO PAPER, HE MADE HIS DEBUT FOR **"THE RED DEVILS"**. THE FORMER MINER STAYED 11 SEASONS WITH **UNITED**, WINNING TWO LEAGUE TITLES AND THE FA CUP, BEFORE RETURNING TO **CITY** IN 1921.

IDENTIFY THESE OTHERS WHO HAVE *"CROSSED THE GREAT DIVIDE"* AND PLAYED FOR BOTH MANCHESTER CLUBS.

1 **ENGLAND** WINGER, SON OF A 1956 FA CUP WINNER, HE WAS VOTED PFA YOUNG PLAYER OF THE YEAR, WON A LEAGUE CUP WITH **CITY** AND PLAYED FOR **UNITED**, **LEEDS UNITED** AND **REAL BETIS**.

2 RIGHT-BACK WHO WON THE 1977 LEAGUE CUP WITH **ASTON VILLA**, TWO FA CUPS WITH **UNITED** IN THE MID-1980S ... AND WAS RELEGATED WITH **CITY**.

3 BORN IN CANADA, HE WON 42 **ENGLAND** CAPS, WON THE UEFA CHAMPIONS LEAGUE WITH BOTH **BAYERN MUNICH** AND **UNITED** AND ENDED HIS PLAYING DAYS WITH A SEASON WITH **CITY**.

4 RUSSIAN WINGER WHO BECAME THE FIRST PLAYER TO SCORE IN EACH OF THE GLASGOW, MERSEYSIDE AND MANCHESTER DERBIES.

5 LOANED OUT BY **UNITED** TO **SUNDERLAND**, **BIRMINGHAM CITY**, **WREXHAM** AND **CITY**, HE JOINED **CITY** IN A £1 MILLION DEAL IN 1999 ... AND THEY THEN LOANED HIM OUT TO **WIGAN ATHLETIC**, **SHEFFIELD WEDNESDAY** AND **GRIMSBY TOWN**. THE MIDFIELDER LATER PLAYED IN THE STATES, AUSTRALIA AND AZERBAIJAN.

6 A 1968 EUROPEAN CUP WINNER WITH **UNITED** WHO PLAYED FOR **CITY** AND **ARSENAL**, HIS STELLAR COACHING CAREER BROUGHT GLORY WITH BOTH **UNITED** AND **CITY**.

7 LAUNCHED HIS CAREER AT **UNITED**, PLAYED IN THE PREMIER LEAGUE FOR **NORWICH CITY** AND **LEICESTER CITY** AND IN THE FOOTBALL LEAGUE WITH **READING, CITY, WALSALL, ROTHERHAM UNITED, BRISTOL CITY** AND **SHEFFIELD WEDNESDAY**. HE HAS ENJOYED SUCCESS IN HIS MANAGEMENT CAREER WITH **COVENTRY CITY**.

8 PROLIFIC STRIKER WHO WON EIGHT MAJOR TROPHIES WITH **UNITED**, INCLUDING THE 1999 TREBLE, AND PLAYED IN THE TOP FLIGHT FOR **ARSENAL, BLACKBURN ROVERS, FULHAM, CITY, PORTSMOUTH** AND **SUNDERLAND**.

9 **UNITED'S** THIRD ALL-TIME TOP GOALSCORER.

10 WINNER OF THREE SOUTH AMERICAN FOOTBALLER OF THE YEAR AWARDS.

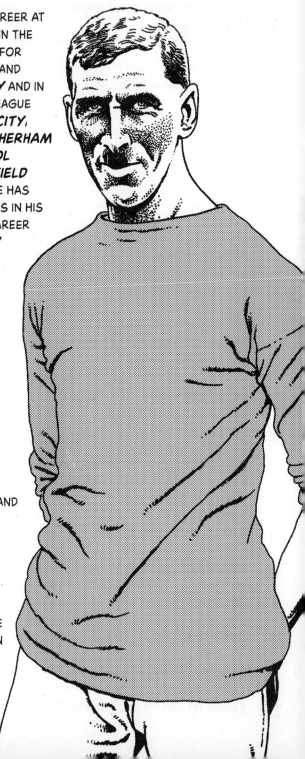

CENTURIONS

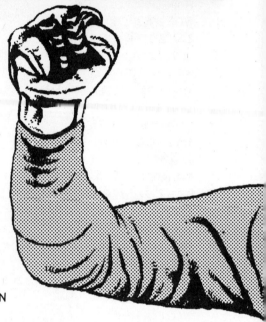

HAVING WON A HUGE NUMBER OF HONOURS WITH **AJAX**, INCLUDING THE UEFA CHAMPIONS LEAGUE, THE UEFA CUP AND FOUR LEAGUE TITLES, **EDWIN VAN DER SAR** JOINED **UNITED** IN 2005. IN SIX SEASONS AT OLD TRAFFORD HE WON A SECOND CHAMPIONS LEAGUE AND FOUR PREMIER LEAGUE TITLES. AT THE TIME OF HIS RETIREMENT, HE WAS THE MOST-CAPPED DUTCH PLAYER OF ALL TIME WITH 130 **NETHERLANDS** APPEARANCES.

IDENTIFY THESE OTHER **UNITED** PLAYERS WHO GAINED MORE THAN 100 INTERNATIONAL CAPS:

1 **DENMARK** (1988 - 2001, 129 CAPS)

2 **UNITED STATES** (2002 - 2017, 121 CAPS)

3 **GERMANY** (2004 - 2016, 121 CAPS)

4 **SWEDEN** (2001 - 2021, 118 CAPS)

5 **REPUBLIC OF IRELAND** (2001 - 2018, 118 CAPS)

6 **CZECH REPUBLIC** (1994 - 2006, 118 CAPS)

7 **URUGUAY** (2002 - 2014, 112 CAPS)

8 **PORTUGAL** (2006 - 2017, 120 CAPS)

9 **MEXICO** (2009 - 2019, 109 CAPS)

10 **SWEDEN** (1993 - 2009, 106 CAPS)

THE UNTOUCHABLE FLEA

HAVING LAUNCHED HIS CAREER IN HIS NATIVE DENMARK WITH *NÆSTVED IF*, *JESPER OLSEN* MADE HIS REPUTATION AT *AJAX*, WHERE HIS ABILITY TO TWIST, TURN AND JUMP TO EVADE TACKLES EARNED HIM THE NICKNAME *"THE FLEA"*. IN HIS THREE SEASONS WITH THE DUTCH CLUB, *OLSEN* -- WHO WAS ALSO KNOWN AS *"THE UNTOUCHABLE"* -- WON TWO EREDIVISIE TITLES AND THE KNVB CUP. HE JOINED *UNITED* IN 1701 AND WON THE FA CUP IN HIS DEBUT SEASON. HE LATER PLAYED IN FRANCE WITH *BORDEAUX* AND *CAEN* BEFORE SETTLING IN AUSTRALIA.

IDENTIFY THESE PLAYERS WHO JOINED *UNITED* FROM DUTCH FOOTBALL:

1 ARRIVED AT *UNITED* IN 2015 AS A LEAGUE AND CUP WINNER -- AND EREDIVISIE TOP SCORER -- WITH *PSV EINDHOVEN* BUT STRUGGLED TO MAKE AN IMPACT. HE MOVED ON TO *LYON* IN 2017 AND JOINED *BARCELONA* IN THE SUMMER OF 2021.

2 LEFT-BACK WHO JOINED *UNITED* FROM *VITESSE ARNHEM* IN 2012, SCORED ON HIS DEBUT BUT FAILED TO NAIL DOWN A REGULAR PLACE. HE MOVED ON TO *SPARTAK MOSCOW* TWO YEARS LATER.

3 SON OF A DUTCH GREAT, WHO WON HONOURS AS AN *AJAX* PLAYER AND MANAGER AND COACHED THE NATIONAL TEAM, HE WON FA CUP, LEAGUE CUP AND UEFA EUROPA LEAGUE HONOURS WITH THE REDS BEFORE RETURNING TO *AJAX* IN 2018 AND TAKING HIS EREDIVISIE TITLE HAUL TO SIX.

4 HAVING WON THE EREDIVISIE TITLE, KNVB CUP AND JOHAN CRUYFF SHIELD WITH *AJAX*, HE SIGNED FOR *UNITED* IN 2020 FOR A REPORTED £35 MILLION WITH £5 MILLION IN ADD-ONS.

5 AN EERSTE DIVISIE WINNER WITH *VITESSE*, HE MOVED TO OLD TRAFFORD IN 1996, PRIMARILY AS A BACK-UP GOALKEEPER, AND MADE 61 APPEARANCES DURING HIS SIX YEARS AT THE CLUB.

6 INJURY PROBLEMS DELAYED HIS TRANSFER FROM *PSV EINDHOVEN* FOR A YEAR BUT FOLLOWING HIS ARRIVAL IN 2001, HE WAS A GOALSCORING MACHINE FOR *UNITED*, WINNING THE PREMIER LEAGUE GOLDEN BOOT IN 2003.

7 CENTRAL DEFENDER WHO JOINED *UNITED*
AS A LEAGUE AND CUP WINNER FROM
PSV EINDHOVEN IN 1998. HE WON
THREE CONSECUTIVE LEAGUE
TITLES -- ONE OF WHICH WAS
PART OF THE HISTORIC 1999
TREBLE -- BEFORE HE WAS
SOLD TO *LAZIO* IN 2001.

DEBUT-IFUL!

A PRODUCT OF **UNITED'S** YOUTH SYSTEM, **MARCUS RASHFORD** BURST ONTO THE NATIONAL STAGE IN EARLY 2016. HE MARKED HIS FIRST TEAM DEBUT WITH TWO GOALS IN THE 5-1 EUROPA LEAGUE VICTORY OVER **MIDTJYLLAND**, AND SCORED TWICE AND MADE THE OTHER IN A 3-2 WIN OVER **ASTON VILLA** ON HIS PREMIER LEAGUE DEBUT THREE DAYS LATER. HE ENDED THE SEASON AN FA CUP WINNER AND CROWNED A STELLAR PERIOD BY SCORING ON HIS **ENGLAND** DEBUT. BEFORE HE CELEBRATED HIS 20TH BIRTHDAY, **RASHFORD** HAD ADDED THE LEAGUE CUP AND UEFA EUROPA LEAGUE TO HIS MEDAL TALLY.

WHICH PLAYERS ANNOUNCED THEIR ARRIVAL IN THE **UNITED** FIRST TEAM WITH THESE MEMORABLE DEBUTS?

1 HAVING LOST HIS FATHER THAT SUMMER, WHICH PLAYER SCORED IN FRONT OF THE STRETFORD END IN AN EMOTIONAL DEBUT IN A 4-0 WIN OVER **CHELSEA** IN 2019?

2 HAVING ARRIVED FROM **EVERTON** THAT SUMMER, WHICH STRIKER OPENED HIS **UNITED** ACCOUNT WITH A GOAL AGAINST **REAL MADRID** IN THE 2017 UEFA SUPER CUP, AND THEN FIVE DAYS LATER, SCORED A BRACE AGAINST **WEST HAM UNITED** ON HIS PREMIER LEAGUE DEBUT?

3 IN HIS 1994 DEBUT, WHICH MIDFIELDER SCORED BOTH GOALS IN A 2-1 VICTORY OVER **PORT VALE** IN THE FOOTBALL LEAGUE CUP, AND ON HIS LEAGUE DEBUT THREE DAYS LATER AWAY TO **IPSWICH TOWN**, SCORED A CONSOLATION GOAL IN A 3-2 DEFEAT?

4 FOLLOWING HIS EXPENSIVE TRANSFER FROM ITALY, WHO SCORED SEVEN MINUTES INTO HIS DEBUT IN 1962?

5 A FIRST DIVISION AND UEFA INTERTOTO CUP CHAMPION WITH **FULHAM**, WHICH FRENCH STRIKER SCORED ON HIS DEBUT IN A 3-2 WIN OVER **SOUTHAMPTON** IN JANUARY, 2004?

6 HAVING SCORED IN THE 2001 2-1 CHARITY SHIELD LOSS TO **LIVERPOOL**, WHICH STRIKER SCORED TWICE IN A 3-2 VICTORY OVER **FULHAM** ON HIS PREMIER LEAGUE DEBUT?

GLOBETROTTERS!

BORN IN ETTERBEEK, BELGIUM TO MOROCCAN PARENTS, *MAROUANE FELLAINI* WAS A BELGIAN FIRST DIVISION WINNER WITH *STANDARD LIÈGE*. HE SPENT FIVE SEASONS WITH *EVERTON* BEFORE JOINING *UNITED* IN 2013, WINNING THE UEFA EUROPA LEAGUE, FA CUP AND LEAGUE CUP BEFORE TAKING HIS TALENTS TO CHINA'S *SHANDONG LUNENG*.

IN WHICH COUNTRIES DID *UNITED* ALUMNI PLAY FOR OR MANAGE THESE TEAMS:

1 *WES BROWN - KERALA BLASTERS* (2017-18)

2 *TERRY COOKE - GABALA* (2010-11)

3 *PETER BARNES - HAMRUN SPARTANS* (1992)

4 *TERRY COOKE - GABALA* (2017-18)

5 *LOUIS VAN GAAL - TELSTAR* (MANAGER, 2021)

6 *GARY BAILEY - KAIZER CHIEFS* (1988-1990)

7 *MIKAËL SILVESTRE - CHENNAIYIN FC* (2014)

8 *RALPH MILNE - SING TAO* (1991-92)

9 *WILF MCGUINNESS - PANACHAIKI* (MANAGER, 1973-75)

10 *FRANK O'FARRELL - AL SHAAB* (MANAGER, 1980)

11 *LEE SHARPE - GRINDAVÍK* (2003)

12 *GEORGE BEST - SEA BEE* (1982)

13 *DAVE GASKELL - ARCADIA SHEPHERDS* (1973-74)

14 *STEVE COPPELL - JAMSHEDPUR* (MANAGER, 2017-18)

THE ITALIAN JOB

AFTER WINNING A LEAGUE TITLE WITH *DANUBIO* IN HIS NATIVE URUGUAY, *EDISON CAVANI* MOVED TO ITALY JUST BEFORE HIS 20TH BIRTHDAY TO PLAY FOR *PALERMO*. HIS NEXT MOVE WAS TO *NAPOLI*, WITH WHOM HE WON THE COPPA ITALIA IN 2011 AND FINISHED SERIE A TOP SCORER THE FOLLOWING SEASON. HE FOUND EVEN GREATER SUCCESS IN FRANCE WITH *PARIS SAINT-GERMAIN* BEFORE JOINING *UNITED* IN 2020.

AS OF THE END OF THE 2020-21 SEASON, WITH WHICH ITALIAN CLUBS HAVE THESE *UNITED* SIGNINGS PLAYED?

1   DAVID BECKHAM

2   DENIS LAW

3   JAAP STAM

4   CHRIS SMALLING

5   AMAD DIALLO

6   LOUIS SAHA

7   RAVEL MORRISON

8   ANDERSON

9   LEE SHARPE

10 PAUL POGBA

11 RAY WILKINS

12 JOE JORDAN

CAVANI

13 *GIUSEPPE ROSSI*

14 *HENRIKH MKHITARYAN*

15 *PATRICE EVRA*

16 *JESPER BLOMQVIST*

17 *KAREL POBORSKÝ*

18 *CARLOS TEVEZ*

19 *JUAN SEBASTIÁN VERÓN*

20 *EDWIN VAN DER SAR*

RED DEVIL DRAGONS

MARK HUGHES WON TWO PREMIER LEAGUE TITLES, FOUR FA CUPS, THREE LEAGUE CUPS AND TWO EUROPEAN CUP WINNERS' CUPS IN A PLAYING CAREER THAT TOOK HIM FROM **UNITED** TO **CHELSEA, EVERTON, SOUTHAMPTON** AND **BLACKBURN ROVERS** AND INCLUDED SPELLS IN SPAIN AND GERMANY. CAPPED 72 TIMES BY **WALES,** HIS FIRST FORAY INTO MANAGEMENT CAME IN 1999 WHEN HE WAS APPOINTED MANAGER OF THE NATIONAL TEAM.

IDENTIFY THESE OTHER **UNITED** PLAYERS CAPPED BY **WALES:**

1 WON THE PREMIER LEAGUE, FA CUP AND EUROPEAN CUP WINNERS' CUP IN THE EARLY 1990S WITH **UNITED,** THE FOOTBALL LEAGUE FIRST DIVISION WITH **MIDDLESBROUGH** IN 1995 AND PLAYED FOR **BARNSLEY, NOTTS COUNTY** AND **BANGOR CITY** .

2 NICKNAMED **"THE LEAP",** A STRIKER WHO PLAYED FOR BOTH MANCHESTER CLUBS IN THE EARLY 1970S, FOLLOWING SPELLS WITH **WREXHAM, BOLTON WANDERERS** AND **NEWCASTLE UNITED.**

3 ONE OF THE GAME'S EARLIEST STARS, HE EXCELLED FOR BOTH MANCHESTER TEAMS AND PLAYED HIS LAST GAME AT THE AGE OF 49 YEARS AND 245 DAYS.

4 MIDFIELDER WHO WON A CROATIAN CUP WITH PRVA HNL SIDE **ISTRA 1961** AND REPRESENTED **WALES** AT EURO 2020.

5 CAPTAIN OF **UNITED'S** 1957 FA YOUTH CUP-WINNING TEAM, HE WAS THE YOUNGEST PLAYER INJURED IN THE MUNICH AIR DISASTER.

6 CAPPED 64 TIMES BY **WALES,** HE WAS APPOINTED NATIONAL TEAM MANAGER IN 2018.

7 HE AVERAGED MORE THAN A GOAL A GAME WITH **NORWICH CITY,** WAS JOINT TOP FLIGHT SCORER WITH **GEORGE BEST** IN 1968 WHILE WITH **SOUTHAMPTON,** AND SIGNED FOR **UNITED** IN 1974.

8   CAPPED 51 TIMES, HE PLAYED FOR *WREXHAM, UNITED, EVERTON, BRIGHTON & HOVE ALBION, STOKE CITY, CHELSEA, WEST BROMWICH ALBION, DERBY COUNTY, SHREWSBURY TOWN* AND *LEEDS UNITED* AND WAS JAILED IN 1993 AFTER BECOMING INVOLVED IN A COUNTERFEIT CURRENCY SCAM.

9   WINGER WHO LAUNCHED HIS CAREER AT *UNITED,* BEFORE PLAYING FOR *NEWCASTLE UNITED, CHARLTON ATHLETIC, CARLISLE UNITED, SWANSEA CITY* (TWO SPELLS) AND *BRADFORD CITY.* SADLY, HE TOOK HIS OWN LIFE IN 1992 AT THE AGE OF 30.

10   WINGER WHO JOINED *UNITED* FROM *SWANSEA CITY* IN 2019 IN A £15 MILLION DEAL.

FIRST AMONG EQUALS

IN HIS SEVEN SEASONS WITH **UNITED**, DURING WHICH TIME HE WON FOUR
PREMIER LEAGUE TITLES, **PARK JI-SUNG** BECAME THE FIRST ASIAN
FOOTBALLER TO WIN THE UEFA CHAMPIONS LEAGUE. HE PLAYED 100 TIMES
FOR **SOUTH KOREA**, INCLUDING APPEARING AT THREE WORLD CUPS.

HE WAS THE FIRST SOUTH KOREAN PLAYER TO PLAY FOR **UNITED**. NAME
THE FIRST PLAYER TO REPRESENT **UNITED** AT SENIOR LEVEL FROM:

1 PORTUGAL (2003)

2 MEXICO (2010)

3 CAMEROON (2003)

4 BULGARIA (2008)

5 SOUTH AFRICA (1999)

6 BRAZIL (2003)

7 ARGENTINA (2001)

8 DENMARK (1984)

9 SERBIA (2006)

10 NETHERLANDS (1982)

11 FRANCE (1992)

12 URUGUAY (2002)

13 ITALY (1965)

14 GERMANY (2015)

15 RUSSIA (1991)

16 COLOMBIA (2014)

GONE GUNNERS!

CHILE'S MOST-CAPPED PLAYER AND THE ALL-TIME TOP GOALSCORER FOR HIS COUNTRY, **ALEXIS SÁNCHEZ** WAS THE FIRST CHILEAN TO PLAY A COMPETITIVE MATCH FOR **UNITED**. SIGNED FROM **ARSENAL** IN 2018, HIS FORM AND CONFIDENCE PLUMMETED AND HIS 2019 EXIT TO SERIE A WAS GREETED WITH RELIEF BY CLUB AND PLAYER.

IDENTIFY THESE OTHER REDS WITH **ARSENAL** CONNECTIONS:

1 FORMER **SHAKHTAR DONETSK** AND **BORUSSIA DORTMUND** MIDFIELDER WHO JOINED **ARSENAL** IN THE SWAP DEAL THAT TOOK **SÁNCHEZ** TO **OLD TRAFFORD**.

2 SIGNED FROM **ARSENAL** FOR £35,000 IN 1961, HE SCORED 145 GOALS IN 265 GAMES FOR **UNITED** BEFORE JOINING **STOKE CITY**.

3 **ENGLAND** INTERNATIONAL WHO WON MULTIPLE HONOURS WITH **UNITED** BUT WHOSE TRANSFER TO **ARSENAL** IN 2014 WAS EXPLAINED BY **LOUIS VAN GAAL** AS A MOVE TO MAKE ROOM FOR **RADAMEL FALCAO**. THE STRIKER DULY SCORED THE QUARTER-FINAL GOAL THAT KNOCKED **UNITED** OUT OF THE 2015 FA CUP.

4 **ALEX FERGUSON'S** FIRST SIGNING, AN **ENGLAND** DEFENDER WHO WON TWO EUROPEAN CUPS, A LEAGUE TITLE AND MORE WITH **NOTTINGHAM FOREST**, THE LEAGUE CUP WITH **ARSENAL** AND THE 1990 FA CUP WITH **UNITED**.

5 CENTRE-HALF WHOSE RUNNING BATTLE WITH **DENIS LAW** IN A 1967 GAME BETWEEN **ARSENAL** AND **UNITED** RESULTED IN SIX-GAME BANS FOR BOTH ... BEFORE THE TWO **SCOTLAND** INTERNATIONALS BECAME TEAMMATES WITH HIS 1969 MOVE TO **UNITED**.

6 THE ALL-TIME TOP SCORER FOR THE **NETHERLANDS** AND TWO-TIME WINNER OF THE PREMIER LEAGUE GOLDEN BOOT.

7   **FRANCE** INTERNATIONAL DEFENDER WHO WON FIVE PREMIER LEAGUE TITLES AND THE UEFA CHAMPIONS LEAGUE WITH **UNITED** BEFORE SIGNING FOR **ARSENAL** IN 2008.

8   1968 EUROPEAN CUP WINNER WHO LATER PLAYED FOR **ARSENAL**, **MANCHESTER CITY**, **EVERTON** AND MORE.

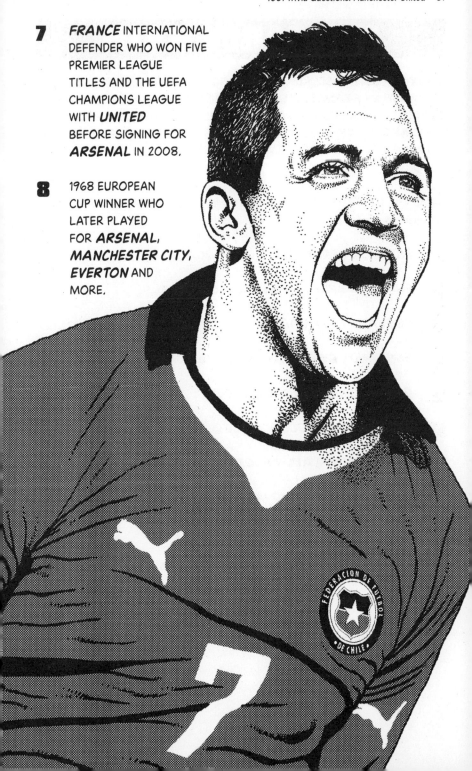

THE EARLY BATH

LAURENT BLANC SCORED THE FIRST GOLDEN GOAL IN WORLD CUP
HISTORY WHEN **FRANCE** DEFEATED **PARAGUAY** 1-0 IN THE ROUND OF 16
EN ROUTE TO WINNING THE WORLD CUP IN 1998. HE FAMOUSLY RECEIVED
THE ONLY RED CARD IN HIS 97 APPEARANCES FOR HIS COUNTRY FOR
SLAPPING **CROATIA'S SLAVEN BILIĆ** IN THE SEMI-FINAL, WHICH RULED
HIM OUT OF THE FINAL.

NAME THE **UNITED** PLAYER RED-CARDED IN THESE INTERNATIONAL
GAMES:

1 **ECUADOR** V **FRANCE**, WORLD CUP, 2018

2 **ENGLAND** V **PORTUGAL**, WORLD CUP, 2006

3 **ENGLAND** V **DENMARK**, NATIONS LEAGUE, 2020

4 **ENGLAND** V **SWEDEN**, WORLD CUP QUALIFIER, 1999

5 **GERMANY** V **CROATIA**, EURO 2008

6 **ENGLAND** V **MOROCCO**, WORLD CUP, 1986

7 **NORTHERN IRELAND** V **SCOTLAND**, HOME INTERNATIONAL, 1970

8 **REPUBLIC OF IRELAND** V **RUSSIA**, FRIENDLY, 1996

9 **ENGLAND** V **ARGENTINA**, WORLD CUP, 1998

10 **ENGLAND** V **SWEDEN**, EUROPEAN CHAMPIONSHIP QUALIFIER, 1998

11 **ARGENTINA** V **CHILE**, COPA AMÉRICA, 2016

12 **AZERBAIJAN** V **NORTHERN IRELAND**,
WORLD CUP QUALIFIER, 2013

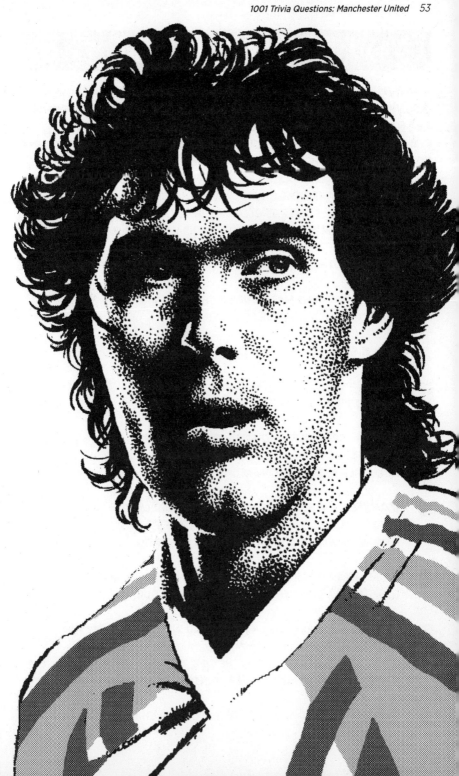

EURO KINGS!

UNITED HAD DRAWN A BLANK IN 213 MINUTES OF FOOTBALL BEFORE **JOHN SIVEBÆK** SCORED THE FIRST GOAL OF **SIR ALEX FERGUSON'S** REIGN IN NOVEMBER, 1986. THE DANISH INTERNATIONAL, WHO HAD REPRESENTED HIS COUNTRY IN THAT SUMMER'S WORLD CUP, WENT ON TO PLAY HIS CLUB FOOTBALL IN FRANCE. HE PLAYED FOR **DENMARK** IN THREE EUROPEAN CHAMPIONSHIPS, INCLUDING THE VICTORIOUS CAMPAIGN THAT MADE THE DANES THE UNLIKELY WINNERS OF EURO 1992, WHEN THE TEAM WAS BROUGHT IN AS AN ELEVENTH-HOUR REPLACEMENT FOR THE BANNED **YUGOSLAVIA** ... AND WENT ON THE WIN THE COMPETITION!

IDENTIFY THESE OTHER EURO WINNERS WITH **UNITED** CONNECTIONS:

1 37-YEAR-OLD WHO MADE ONE OF THE GOALS THAT GAVE HIS COUNTRY VICTORY IN THE EURO 1988 FINAL.

2 **SIVEBÆK'S** TEAMMATE IN **DENMARK'S** 1992 SQUAD.

3 WEEKS AFTER JOINING **UNITED** AS THE WORLD'S MOST EXPENSIVE GOALKEEPER, HE WAS A WINNER AT EURO 2000.

4 CENTRAL DEFENDER WHO SCORED HIS COUNTRY'S FIRST GOAL OF THE EURO 2000 TOURNAMENT, HE RETIRED FROM INTERNATIONAL FOOTBALL AFTER VICTORY IN THE FINAL.

5 **BARCELONA** STAR WHO HAD WON PREMIER LEAGUE AND CHAMPIONS LEAGUE HONOURS WITH **UNITED**, HE PLAYED EVERY MINUTE OF **SPAIN'S** UEFA EURO 2012 CAMPAIGN.

6 A 2010 WORLD CUP AND 2012 EUROPEAN CHAMPIONSHIP WINNER DESPITE NOT PLAYING A MINUTE IN EITHER TOURNAMENT.

7 A **CHELSEA** PLAYER WHEN HE SCORED IN THE EURO 2012 FINAL.

8 HE SCORED THREE GOALS IN THE 2012 TOURNAMENT AND TOOK THE ARMBAND IN THE FINAL WHEN THE INJURED CAPTAIN WAS REPLACED.

9 2016 SILVER BOOT-WINNING CAPTAIN OF THE CHAMPIONS.

RAY "BUTCH" WILKINS

CAPPED 84 TIMES BY *ENGLAND*, FOR WHOM HE APPEARED AT EURO 1980 AND THE 1982 AND 1986 WORLD CUPS, *RAY WILKINS* PLAYED AT THE HIGHEST LEVEL IN ENGLAND, ITALY, FRANCE AND SCOTLAND. FOLLOWING HIS DEATH IN 2018 AT THE AGE OF 61, FLOWERS WERE LAID AT HIS SHIRT PITCHSIDE BY *FRANCO BARESI*, HIS FORMER CAPTAIN AT *AC MILAN*, AND THE FANS HELD ALOFT A BANNER THAT READ "*CIAO RAY: LEGGENDA ROSSONERA*" -- ("GOODBYE RAY: LEGEND OF THE RED AND BLACKS").

1 HE CAPTAINED WHICH LONDON SIDE TO PROMOTION BACK TO THE TOP FLIGHT IN 1977, BEFORE THEY WERE RELEGATED AGAIN TWO YEARS LATER?

2 WHO WAS THE MANAGER WHO SIGNED HIM TO *UNITED* IN 1979?

3 HE PLAYED IN THE SAME *AC MILAN* TEAM AS WHICH *ENGLAND* STRIKER, WHO ALSO JOINED THE ITALIANS IN THE SUMMER OF 1984?

4 IN 1987, *WILKINS* PLAYED BRIEFLY FOR WHICH FRENCH CLUB?

5 WHO WAS THE MANAGER WHO SIGNED *WILKINS* TO *RANGERS* IN NOVEMBER, 1987?

6 *WILKINS* HAD TWO LENGTHY SPELLS AT WHICH LONDON CLUB -- BROKEN BY A BRIEF PERIOD AT *CRYSTAL PALACE* -- THE SECOND OF WHICH SAW HIM INSTALLED AS PLAYER/MANAGER?

7 *WILKINS* MANAGED *FULHAM* IN THE 1997-98 SEASON -- NAME THE *ENGLAND* TEAMMATE WHO SUCCEEDED HIM AS CLUB BOSS.

8 HE WAS ASSISTANT MANAGER TO *GIANLUCA VIALLI* AT *CHELSEA* AND WHICH OTHER CLUB?

9 WHICH MIDDLE EASTERN NATIONAL TEAM DID HE MANAGE, LEADING THEM TO THE 2015 AFC ASIAN CUP TOURNAMENT?

10 IN 2015, *WILKINS* WAS ASSISTANT MANGER TO *TIM SHERWOOD* AT WHICH PREMIER LEAGUE CLUB?

ROONEY'S RECORD

ON 8 SEPTEMBER 2015, **WAYNE ROONEY** BROKE **BOBBY CHARLTON'S ENGLAND** GOALSCORING RECORD, NETTING HIS 50TH INTERNATIONAL GOAL FROM A PENALTY IN A EURO 2016 QUALIFYING MATCH AGAINST **SWITZERLAND**, AT WEMBLEY, IN HIS 107TH APPEARANCE FOR HIS COUNTRY. **CHARLTON'S** RECORD HAD STOOD FOR 45 YEARS. BY THE TIME HE RETIRED FROM INTERNATIONAL FOOTBALL, **ROONEY** HAD TAKEN HIS TALLY TO 53 GOALS IN 120 APPEARANCES.

AS OF THE SUMMER OF 2021, WHICH PAST OR PRESENT **UNITED** PLAYERS HOLD THE GOALSCORING RECORD FOR THESE COUNTRIES?

1 BELGIUM

2 PORTUGAL

3 NETHERLANDS

4 MEXICO

5 BULGARIA

6 CHILE

7 NORTHERN IRELAND

8 COLOMBIA

9 SCOTLAND

10 ARMENIA

11 SWEDEN

CARDIFF CONNECTIONS

FEDERICO MACHEDA MADE ONE OF THE MOST MEMORABLE DEBUTS IN PREMIER LEAGUE HISTORY. WITH **UNITED** TRAILING **ASTON VILLA** 2-1 IN 2009, THE 17-YEAR-OLD ITALIAN REPLACED **NANI** AROUND THE HOUR MARK. **CRISTIANO RONALDO** LEVELLED THE SCORES AND THE GAME WAS HEADING FOR A DRAW -- UNTIL THE THIRD MINUTE OF INJURY TIME, WHEN **MACHEDA** STRUCK TO WIN THE GAME IN DRAMATIC FASHION. HIS SUBSEQUENT **UNITED** CAREER FAILED TO MATCH THAT FANTASTIC START AND, FOLLOWING A SERIES OF LOANS, HE SIGNED FOR **CARDIFF CITY** IN 2014. HE EVENTUALLY SETTLED AT **PANATHINAIKOS** IN 2018.

IDENTIFY THESE OTHER REDS WITH **CARDIFF CITY** CONNECTIONS:

1 HAVING PLAYED WITH HIS TWIN BROTHER AT **UNITED**, HE JOINED **CARDIFF CITY** IN EARLY 2014 FOLLOWING A LOAN SPELL WITH **QUEENS PARK RANGERS**. HE SUBSEQUENTLY PLAYED FOR **MIDDLESBROUGH** BEFORE SIGNING FOR **NANTES** IN 2018.

2 ACADEMY GRADUATE WHO HAD LOAN SPELLS WITH **ROYAL ANTWERP**, **HULL CITY** AND **TOTTENHAM HOTSPUR** BEFORE SIGNING FOR **SUNDERLAND** IN 2009. AFTER A PROMOTION-WINNING CAMPAIGN WITH **CARDIFF**, HE MOVED ON TO **CRYSTAL PALACE**, THEN BACK TO **HULL CITY** BEFORE SIGNING FOR **HUDDERSFIELD TOWN** IN 2019.

3 MANAGER WHO HAD SPELLS IN CHARGE OF **UNITED** AND **CARDIFF**, AS WELL AS **LEICESTER CITY**, **WEYMOUTH**, **TORQUAY UNITED**, **AL-SHAAB** AND THE **IRAN** NATIONAL TEAM.

4 FORWARD WHO HAS SPENT MOST OF HIS CAREER WITH **CRYSTAL PALACE**, MUCH OF HIS BRIEF SPELL WITH **UNITED** WAS SPENT ON LOAN AT **CARDIFF CITY**.

5 A PRODUCT OF THE *UNITED* ACADEMY, A MIDFIELDER WHO WON PROMOTION AND THEN THE PREMIER LEAGUE WITH *LEICESTER CITY*, WON THE FA CUP WITH *CHELSEA* AND HAS SPENT TIME ON LOAN AT *HUDDERSFIELD TOWN*, *CARDIFF CITY*, *WATFORD*, *BARNSLEY*, *BURNLEY* AND *ASTON VILLA*.

6 UNABLE TO BREAK INTO THE *CARDIFF* FIRST TEAM, HE JOINED *UNITED* IN 1952 AND WON A LEAGUE TITLE IN 1956. HE MISSED THE TRIP THAT ENDED IN DISASTER AT MUNICH AND PLAYED IN THE 1958 FA CUP FINAL. HE WAS TOP SCORER AT *SWANSEA CITY* AND ENDED HIS PLAYING DAYS AT *NEWPORT COUNTY*.

7 *ENGLAND* GOALKEEPER WHO HAS PLAYED WITH NUMEROUS CLUBS, WON HONOURS WITH *CARDIFF CITY* AND *BURNLEY* AND RETURNED TO *UNITED* IN 2021 AFTER 11 YEARS AWAY.

8 *UNITED* GOALSCORING LEGEND WHOSE SECOND JOB IN MANAGEMENT WAS WITH *CARDIFF CITY* IN 2014.

9 ACADEMY GRADUATE WHO SIGNED FOR *WEST HAM UNITED* IN 2012, PLAYED FOR *QUEENS PARK RANGERS*, *CARDIFF* AND MORE, INCLUDING CLUBS IN ITALY, MEXICO, SWEDEN AND NETHERLANDS, HE HAS BEEN A *JAMAICA* INTERNATIONAL SINCE 2020.

TURKEY TRAVELS

IN EIGHT SEASONS AT *OLD TRAFFORD*, FORMER *SPORTING CP* STAR *NANI* WON FOUR PREMIER LEAGUE TITLES, TWO LEAGUE CUPS, THE UEFA CHAMPIONS LEAGUE AND THE FIFA CLUB WORLD CUP. THE *PORTUGAL* STAR SUBSEQUENTLY SPENT TIME BACK AT *SPORTING CP*, PLAYED IN TURKEY WITH *FENERBAHÇE*, IN SPAIN WITH *VALENCIA* AND IN ITALY WITH *LAZIO*, BEFORE JOINING *ORLANDO CITY* IN 2018.

IDENTIFY THESE OTHERS WHO PLAYED IN TURKEY:

1 2002 WORLD CUP WINNER WITH *BRAZIL*, HE WON THE FA CUP WITH *UNITED* IN 2004 AND THE 2006 TURKISH CUP WITH *BEŞIKTAŞ*.

2 ALL-TIME *NETHERLANDS* TOP GOALSCORER WHO PLAYED ALONGSIDE *NANI* AT *UNITED* AND *FENERBAHÇE*.

3 PLAYED FOR *UNITED* ALONGSIDE HIS TWIN BROTHER, SPENT FIVE YEARS AT *LYON*, SIGNED FOR *İSTANBUL BAŞAKŞEHIR* IN 2020.

4 FRENCH WINGER WHO JOINED *UNITED* FROM *BORDEAUX*, HE SPENT FIVE SEASONS WITH *NEWCASTLE UNITED*, A FEW MONTHS WITH *WIGAN ATHLETIC*, PLAYED IN RUSSIA AND BULGARIA AND SIGNED FOR TURKEY'S *BB ERZURUMSPOR* IN 2019.

5 *UNITED'S* FIRST JAPANESE PLAYER, HE SPENT TIME ON LOAN FROM *BORUSSIA DORTMUND* AT *BEŞIKTAŞ* IN 2019.

6 *NORWAY* INTERNATIONAL DEFENDER WHO JOINED *UNITED* FROM *BEŞIKTAŞ* IN 1996.

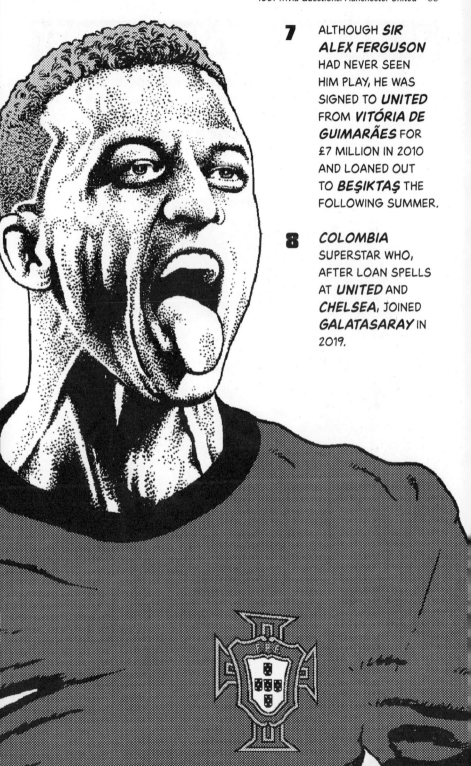

7 ALTHOUGH *SIR ALEX FERGUSON* HAD NEVER SEEN HIM PLAY, HE WAS SIGNED TO *UNITED* FROM *VITÓRIA DE GUIMARÃES* FOR £7 MILLION IN 2010 AND LOANED OUT TO *BEŞIKTAŞ* THE FOLLOWING SUMMER.

8 *COLOMBIA* SUPERSTAR WHO, AFTER LOAN SPELLS AT *UNITED* AND *CHELSEA*, JOINED *GALATASARAY* IN 2019.

JAWS AND THE JULES RIMET

THE FIRST **SCOTLAND** PLAYER TO SCORE IN THREE WORLD CUPS -- IN 1974, 1978 AND 1982 -- **JOE JORDAN** WAS A FEARSOME STRIKER WHO JOINED **UNITED** FROM **LEEDS UNITED** IN 1978. HAVING LOST HIS TWO FRONT TEETH EARLY IN HIS CAREER AFTER BEING KICKED IN THE FACE DURING A GOALMOUTH SCRAMBLE, HE BORE THE NICKNAME **"JAWS"**.

1 WHICH *UNITED* GOALKEEPER IS THE ONLY PLAYER TO FEATURE IN FOUR *SCOTLAND* WORLD CUP SQUADS -- IN THE 1982, 1986, 1990 AND 1998 TOURNAMENTS?

2 WHICH *MANCHESTER UNITED MANAGER* REPRESENTED *SCOTLAND* IN TWO WORLD CUP TOURNAMENTS?

3 BESIDES *JORDAN*, HOW MANY OF THE FIVE OTHER PLAYERS IN *SCOTLAND'S* 1974 WORLD CUP SQUAD WHO WERE PAST, PRESENT OR FUTURE *UNITED* PLAYERS CAN YOU NAME? *(THREE WERE UNITED PLAYERS AT THE TIME, ONE HAD MOVED ON TO MANCHESTER CITY AND THE OTHER WAS A TEAMMATE OF JORDAN AT LEEDS UNITED IN 1974.)*

4 WHICH *UNITED* STAR, WHO HAD PREVIOUSLY WON FOUR LEAGUE TITLES WITH *CELTIC* AND WOULD GO ON TO WIN MANAGERIAL HONOURS WITH *SWINDON TOWN, BIRMINGHAM CITY* AND *STOKE CITY*, WAS A MEMBER OF THE 1978 *SCOTLAND* SQUAD?

5 WITH THE DEATH OF *JOCK STEIN*, WHICH SUBSEQUENT *UNITED* LEGEND STEPPED UP TO MANAGE *SCOTLAND* AND STEER HIS COUNTRY TO THE 1986 WORLD CUP?

6 WHICH *UNITED* PLAYER SCORED FOR *SCOTLAND* IN THE 1986 WORLD CUP GAME AGAINST *WEST GERMANY*?

7 WHICH *UNITED* FULL-BACK MADE ONE APPEARANCE FOR *SCOTLAND* AT THE 1986 WORLD CUP?

8 WHICH GOALKEEPER, WHO WOULD LATER SPEND A BRIEF PERIOD ON LOAN WITH *UNITED* IN 2001, WAS A MEMBER OF *SCOTLAND'S* 1986 AND 1990 WORLD CUP SQUADS?

"LIFE IS SO GOOD IN AMERICA ..."

THE FIRST ENGLISH PLAYER TO WIN LEAGUE TITLES IN FOUR COUNTRIES -- ENGLAND, SPAIN, THE UNITED STATES AND FRANCE -- *DAVID BECKHAM* WON TWO MLS CUPS WITH *LA GALAXY.* HE IS NOW ONE OF THE OWNERS OF MLS FRANCHISE TEAM *INTER MIAMI CF. ZLATAN IBRAHIMOVIĆ* IS ANOTHER *UNITED* STAR TO HAVE PLAYED FOR *LA GALAXY.*

WITH WHICH NORTH AMERICAN TEAMS DID THE FOLLOWING PLAY?

1   GEORGE BEST

2   WAYNE ROONEY

3   BASTIAN SCHWEINSTEIGER

4   BRIAN KIDD

5   PETER BEARDSLEY

6   ALEX STEPNEY

7   GIUSEPPE ROSSI

8   JIM HOLTON

9   TONY DUNNE

10   JAVIER HERNÁNDEZ

11   GEORGE GRAHAM

12   IAN STOREY-MOORE

13   JIMMY NICHOLL

RED CELEBS

STAR OF TV'S *"LOVEJOY"* AND *"DEADWOOD"*, IAN MCSHANE'S FILM ROLES RANGE FROM *TAI LUNG* IN *"KUNG FU PANDA"* TO *BLACKBEARD* IN *"PIRATES OF THE CARIBBEAN: ON STRANGER TIDES"*. THE GOLDEN GLOBE-WINNING ACTOR -- WHO PLAYED A FADING FOOTBALL STAR, OPPOSITE *ADAM FAITH*, IN THE 1979 FILM *"YESTERDAY'S HERO "* -- IS A LIFELONG RED. THAT'S HARDLY SURPRISING, AS HE IS THE SON OF FOOTBALLER *HARRY MCSHANE*, WHO WON A LEAGUE TITLE WITH *UNITED* IN 1952 AND LATER WORKED AS A SCOUT AND STADIUM ANNOUNCER FOR THE CLUB.

IDENTIFY THESE OTHER CELEBRITY REDS:

1 *MARTIN MOSCROP* AND *DONALD JOHNSON* ARE *UNITED* FANS AND BASSIST *JEZ KERR* PLAYED IN *UNITED'S* YOUTH TEAM -- THEY PLAY TOGETHER IN WHICH LEGENDARY *FACTORY RECORDS* BAND?

2 FOUNDER AND LEAD SINGER OF *SIMPLY RED*.

3 A MEMBER OF POP GROUP *HEAR'SAY*, SHE PLAYED *MICHELLE CONNOR* ON *"CORONATION STREET"*.

4 IRISH ACTOR WHOSE TV CREDITS INCLUDE *"COLD FEET"*, *"MURPHY'S LAW"* AND *"STAN LEE'S LUCKY MAN"*.

5 ACTOR WHO PLAYED *GAZ WILKINSON* IN *"TWO PINTS OF LAGER AND A PACKET OF CRISPS"* AND *DC SPIKE TANNER* IN *"NO OFFENCE"*.

6   LEAD SINGER WITH *THE STONE ROSES*.

7   JAMAICAN SPRINTER, AN EIGHT-TIME OLYMPIC GOLD MEDALLIST.

8   GOLFER WHO WON THE 2011 US OPEN, THE 2012 PGA CHAMPIONSHIP, THE 2014 OPEN CHAMPIONSHIP, AND THE 2014 PGA CHAMPIONSHIP.

9   *"THIS MORNING"* TV SHOW PRESENTER.

10   ACTOR WHOSE CREDITS RANGE FROM TV'S *"OUR FRIENDS IN THE NORTH"*, *"CRACKER"* AND *"DOCTOR WHO"*, TO SUCH MOVIES AS *"SHALLOW GRAVE"* AND *"THOR: THE DARK WORLD"*.

11   TV PRESENTER, CO-FOUNDER OF *FACTORY RECORDS* AND CO-OWNER OF MANCHESTER'S *HAÇIENDA* NIGHTCLUB, HE DIED IN 2007.

BIG DUNC AND THE BOYS

A DYNAMIC MIDFIELDER KNOWN AS *"BIG DUNC"* OR *"THE TANK"*, HE
WAS NICKNAMED *"BOOM BOOM"* IN THE GERMAN PRESS FOR *"THE BIG
BERTHA SHOT IN HIS BOOTS"*. THOSE WHO SAW HIM PLAY -- AND THOSE
WHO PLAYED ALONGSIDE HIM -- SAY THAT *DUNCAN EDWARDS* MAY BE
THE GREATEST FOOTBALLER THAT ENGLAND EVER PRODUCED. TWO WEEKS
AFTER THE 1958 MUNICH AIR DISASTER, THE 21-YEAR-OLD SUCCUMBED TO
THE TERRIBLE INJURIES HE HAD RECEIVED IN THE CRASH.

ON FEBRUARY 6, 1958, THE PLANE BRINGING *UNITED'S* TEAM HOME
FROM A EUROPEAN CUP GAME IN BELGRADE CRASHED ON TAKE-OFF
AFTER REFUELLING IN MUNICH. 23 OF THE 44 PEOPLE ON BOARD BRITISH
EUROPEAN AIRWAYS FLIGHT 609 WERE KILLED, INCLUDING TWO CREW, TWO
PASSENGERS, EIGHT JOURNALISTS AND THREE *UNITED* STAFF MEMBERS.
EIGHT PLAYERS LOST THEIR LIVES: *EDWARDS, GEOFF BENT, ROGER
BYRNE, EDDIE COLMAN, MARK JONES, DAVID PEGG, TOMMY
TAYLOR* AND *LIAM "BILLY" WHELAN*. MANAGER *MATT BUSBY*
RECOVERED FROM CRITICAL INJURIES TO REBUILD THE TEAM.

IDENTIFY THESE PLAYERS WHO SURVIVED:

1   WORLD CUP WINNER, KNIGHTED IN 1994.

2   *UNITED'S* GOALKEEPER IN THE 1957 FA CUP FINAL.

3   *UNITED'S* GOALKEEPER IN THE 1958 FA CUP FINAL.

4   *NORTHERN IRELAND* HALF-BACK, HE NEVER PLAYED AGAIN.

5   18-YEAR-OLD WINGER, THE YOUNGEST PLAYER IN THE CRASH. HE
     JOINED HOMETOWN CLUB *SWANSEA CITY* IN 1961.

6   WINGER WHO SUFFERED A FRACTURED SKULL, BROKEN LEG
     AND KIDNEY DAMAGE, BUT RECOVERED AND LATER PLAYED FOR
     NEWCASTLE UNITED, LINCOLN CITY AND *MANSFIELD TOWN*.

7   HE SUBSEQUENTLY WON HONOURS WITH *STOKE CITY* BEFORE AN
     EXTENSIVE PLAYING AND COACHING CAREER IN THE STATES.

8 FORMER ***BIRMINGHAM CITY*** WINGER WHO SPENT TWO MONTHS IN HOSPITAL IN GERMANY AFTER THE CRASH AND NEVER PLAYED AGAIN.

9 HE ASSUMED THE CAPTAINCY FOLLOWING THE LOSS OF ***ROGER BYRNE*** AND PLAYED EVERY GAME OF ***UNITED'S*** 1959-60 SEASON.

"THE KING OF KINGS"

ONE OF THE ALL-TIME GREAT SWEDISH STRIKERS, NICKNAMED *"THE KING OF KINGS"* BY ADORING *CELTIC* FANS, *HENRIK LARSSON* WON HONOURS IN THE NETHERLANDS, SCOTLAND, SWEDEN, SPAIN AND ENGLAND.

1 HIS GOALSCORING EXPLOITS IN SWEDEN WITH *HÖGABORG* AND *HELSINGBORG* EARNED HIM A 1993 TRANSFER TO WHICH DUTCH CLUB, WITH WHOM HE WOULD WIN TWO KNVB CUPS?

2 IN HIS SEVEN SEASONS WITH *CELTIC* BETWEEN 1997 AND 2004, *LARSSON* WON FOUR LEAGUE TITLES, TWO SCOTTISH CUPS AND TWO SCOTTISH LEAGUE CUPS. HOW MANY OF THE FOUR MANAGERS AND ONE CARETAKER MANAGER UNDER WHOM HE PLAYED CAN YOU NAME?

3 HE WON THE EUROPEAN GOLDEN BOOT IN 2001, THE AWARD GIVEN TO THE OVERALL TOP SCORER IN EUROPEAN LEAGUES. TWO OTHER *UNITED* ALUMNI HAVE WON THAT AWARD -- CAN YOU NAME THEM?

4 HE JOINED *BARCELONA* IN 2004 AND WON LA LIGA IN BOTH OF THE TWO SEASONS HE WAS WITH THE CLUB, AS WELL AS THE 2006 UEFA CHAMPIONS LEAGUE. WHO DID *BARCELONA* BEAT IN THAT CHAMPIONS LEAGUE FINAL?

5 WHO WAS THE MANAGER WHO STEERED **BARCELONA** TO THOSE LEAGUE AND CHAMPIONS LEAGUE TRIUMPHS?

6 **LARSSON** WON HIS SECOND GULDBOLLEN -- THE AWARD GIVEN TO THE SWEDISH PLAYER OF THE YEAR -- IN 2004. NAME THE TWO OTHER **UNITED** PLAYERS TO WIN THAT AWARD.

7 **LARSSON** RETURNED TO SWEDEN AND **HELSINGBORG** BEFORE JOINING **UNITED** ON JANUARY 1, 2007. HE LEFT THE CLUB TWO MONTHS LATER -- WHICH TROPHY DID **UNITED** WIN THAT SEASON?

8 HAVING COACHED AND MANAGED A NUMBER OF TEAMS IN SWEDEN, **LARSSON** WAS APPOINTED ASSISTANT MANAGER OF WHICH EUROPEAN GIANT IN 2020?

CROSSING THE BORDER

THE FIRST PLAYER IN HISTORY TO SCORE IN EACH OF THE GLASGOW, MERSEYSIDE AND MANCHESTER LOCAL DERBIES, *ANDREI KANCHELSKIS* WAS CAPPED INTERNATIONALLY BY THE *SOVIET UNION, CIS* AND *RUSSIA*. HE WON TWO LEAGUE TITLES, BOTH DOMESTIC CUPS AND THE EUROPEAN SUPER CUP WITH *UNITED* BUT A STRAINED RELATIONSHIP WITH *SIR ALEX FERGUSON*, AGAINST A BACKDROP OF THE CLUB'S UNEASE WITH HIS AGENTS, SAW HIM SOLD TO *EVERTON* IN 1995.

KANCHELSKIS IS ONE OF THE FEW PLAYERS TO HAVE WON THE ENGLISH PREMIER LEAGUE AND THE SCOTTISH PREMIER LEAGUE. IDENTIFY THESE OTHER *UNITED* PLAYERS WHO HAVE MATCHED THAT FEAT:

1 SWEDISH STRIKER WHO WON IN SCOTLAND WITH *CELTIC* IN 1997-98, 2000-01, 2001-02 AND 2003-04 AND WITH *UNITED* IN 2006-07.

2 NICKNAMED *"CHOCCY"*, HE WON THE TITLE WITH *CELTIC* IN 1985-86 AND FOUR PREMIER LEAGUES WITH *UNITED* BEFORE JOINING *MOTHERWELL* IN 1998.

3 IRISH MIDFIELDER WHO WON A LEAGUE TITLE WITH *CELTIC* IN 2005-06 TO ADD TO THE SEVEN LEAGUE TITLES HE WON WITH *UNITED*.

4 AFTER WINNING FIVE LEAGUE TITLES WITH *RANGERS* BETWEEN 1992 AND 1997, THIS GOALKEEPER WON A LEAGUE TITLE WITH *UNITED* IN 2001 DESPITE ONLY PLAYING IN TWO LEAGUE GAMES.

5 A PREMIER LEAGUE WINNER WITH *UNITED* IN 1992-93, HE SPENT SIX YEARS AT *ASTON VILLA* -- WITH WHOM HE WON THE PREMIER LEAGUE GOLDEN BOOT -- BEFORE WINNING A LEAGUE TITLE WITH *CELTIC* IN THE 2005-06 SEASON.

OUTGOING INCOME

LOCAL LAD **DENNIS VIOLETT** CAME THROUGH THE JUNIOR RANKS AT **OLD TRAFFORD** TO ESTABLISH HIMSELF IN THE TEAM KNOWN AS **"THE BUSBY BABES"**. HE WON TWO LEAGUE TITLES AND, AFTER SURVIVING THE MUNICH AIR DISASTER, HIT A CLUB RECORD 32 GOALS IN 36 LEAGUE GAMES IN THE 1959-60 SEASON. HE MADE HIS **ENGLAND** DEBUT SHORTLY AFTER, SO IT WAS SOMEWHAT SURPRISING THAT **BUSBY** SOLD THE 28-YEAR-OLD TO **STOKE CITY** IN A £25,000 DEAL IN EARLY 1962. **STOKE'S** INVESTMENT SOON PAID OFF, AS THEY WERE PROMOTED BACK TO THE TOP FLIGHT THE FOLLOWING SEASON AND REACHED THE 1964 LEAGUE CUP FINAL.

WHICH CLUBS DID THE FOLLOWING JOIN FROM **UNITED:**

1 1972: **FRANCIS BURNS**, £50,000

2 1972: **ALAN GOWLING**, £60,000

3 1973: **TED MACDOUGALL**, £130,000

4 1978: **GORDON HILL**, £250,000

5 1979: **BRIAN GREENHOFF**, £50,000

6 1980: **ANDY RITCHIE**, £500,000

7 1984: **RAY WILKINS**, £1,500,000

8 1986: ***MARK HUGHES***, £2,500,000

9 1995: ***PAUL INCE***, £7,000,000

10 2001: ***JAAP STAM***, £15,250,000

11 2015: ***ÁNGEL DI MARÍA***, £44,000,000

12 2016: ***PAUL POGBA***, £89,300,000

CAPTAINS FANTASTIC

BRYAN ROBSON MADE 90 APPEARANCES FOR *ENGLAND*, 65 OF THEM AS CAPTAIN. HE LED HIS COUNTRY INTO TWO WORLD CUPS AND A EUROPEAN CHAMPIONSHIP, ALTHOUGH HIS TOURNAMENT APPEARANCES WERE CURTAILED BY INJURY. WHEN HE CAPTAINED *UNITED* TO VICTORY IN THE 1983 FA CUP FINAL HE WAS THE FIRST ENGLISHMAN TO LIFT THE TROPHY FOR *UNITED* SINCE *CHARLIE ROBERTS* IN 1909. *ROBSON* WENT ON TO CAPTAIN THE SIDES THAT WON THE FA CUP IN 1985 AND 1990 AND THE EUROPEAN CUP WINNERS' CUP IN 1991.

NAME THESE OTHER CUP-WINNING *UNITED* CAPTAINS:

1 1948 FA CUP FINAL

2 1963 FA CUP FINAL

3 1968 EUROPEAN CUP FINAL

4 1977 FA CUP FINAL

5 1991 EUROPEAN SUPER CUP

6 1992 LEAGUE CUP FINAL

7 1994 FA CUP FINAL

8 1996 FA CUP FINAL

9 1999 FA CUP FINAL.

10 1999 UEFA CHAMPIONS LEAGUE FINAL

11 1999 INTERCONTINENTAL CUP

12 2004 FA CUP FINAL

13 2006 LEAGUE CUP FINAL

14 2008 UEFA CHAMPIONS LEAGUE FINAL

15 2008 FIFA CLUB WORLD CUP

16 2009 LEAGUE CUP FINAL

17 2010 LEAGUE CUP FINAL

18 2016 FA CUP FINAL

19 2017 LEAGUE CUP FINAL

20 2017 UEFA EUROPA LEAGUE FINAL

COME TOGETHER

SIGNED FROM **PSV EINDHOVEN** IN 1998, **JAAP STAM** WON THREE PREMIER LEAGUE TITLES, INCLUDING THE 1999 TREBLE OF LEAGUE, FA CUP AND UEFA CHAMPIONS LEAGUE. NAME THE CLUBS FROM WHICH THESE MEMBERS OF THAT CHAMPIONS OF EUROPE TEAM JOIN **UNITED**:

1   *PETER SCHMEICHEL*

2   *RONNY JOHNSEN*

3   *DENIS IRWIN*

4   *JESPER BLOMQVIST*

5   *DWIGHT YORKE*

6   *ANDY COLE*

7   *TEDDY SHERINGHAM*

8   *OLE GUNNAR SOLSKJÆR*

DAD AND LAD

HAVING WON LEAGUE AND THE COPA LIBERTADORES IN HIS NATIVE ARGENTINA WITH *ESTUDIANTES*, *JUAN SEBASTIÁN VERÓN* PLAYED ALONGSIDE *DIEGO MARADONA* AT *BOCA JUNIORS*. IN 1996, *SVEN-GÖRAN ERIKSSON* TOOK HIM TO *SAMPDORIA*, AND HIS TIME IN ITALY SAW HIM WIN THE COPPA ITALIA AND UEFA CUP IN HIS ONE SEASON WITH *PARMA*, AND THE SCUDETTO, COPPA ITALIA AND ITALIAN SUPER CUP WITH *LAZIO*. HE MADE HIS DEBUT FOR *LAZIO* IN A 1-0 VICTORY OVER *UNITED* IN THE EUROPEAN SUPER CUP. FOLLOWING DISMAL SPELLS WITH *UNITED* AND *CHELSEA*, HE FOUND SUCCESS WITH *INTERNAZIONALE* BEFORE CONTINUING HIS CAREER BACK HOME IN ARGENTINA.

JUAN IS THE ELDEST SON OF FORMER *ARGENTINA* STRIKER *JUAN RAMÓN VERÓN*, WHO SCORED FOR *ESTUDIANTES* AGAINST *UNITED* AT *OLD TRAFFORD* IN THE 1968 INTERCONTINENTAL CUP. IDENTIFY THESE OTHER FOOTBALLING FATHERS AND SONS WITH LINKS TO *UNITED*:

1 SON OF A WINGER WHO WON THE LEAGUE AND FA CUP WITH *MANCHESTER CITY*, AT THE OUTSET OF HIS CAREER HE PLAYED ALONGSIDE HIS FATHER FOR *STOCKPORT COUNTY*.

2 SON OF AN INTERNATIONAL FOOTBALLER WHOSE NICKNAME TRANSLATES TO *"PEA"* -- A REFERENCE TO HIS STRIKING GREEN EYES -- HIS NICKNAME MEANS *"LITTLE PEA"*.

3 SON OF A TRIPLE BALLON D'OR AND WORLD CUP GOLDEN BALL WINNER, HE PLAYED UNDER HIS FATHER AT *BARCELONA*.

4 ***ENGLAND*** LEFT-BACK WHO WON THE 1948 FA CUP WITH ***UNITED***, HIS SON WAS A LEAGUE AND EUROPEAN CUP WINNER WITH THE REDS

5 HE PLAYED UNDER HIS MANAGER DAD AT ***UNITED*** AND HAD LENGTHY SPELLS AT ***WOLVES*** AND ***WREXHAM***, BEFORE GOING INTO MANAGEMENT AT ***PETERBOROUGH UNITED***.

6 WON NUMEROUS HONOURS AS A ***UNITED*** PLAYER BEFORE ENJOYING A LONG CAREER IN MANAGEMENT THAT SAW HIS SON PLAY UNDER HIM AT ***BIRMINGHAM CITY*** AND ***HULL CITY***.

7 A GOALKEEPER LIKE HIS DAD WHO PLAYED FOR ***IPSWICH TOWN*** AND ***CRYSTAL PALACE***, HE WON TWO FA CUPS WITH ***UNITED***.

8 STAR STRIKER WHOSE SON, ***DEVANTE***, STARTED HIS CAREER AT ***MANCHESTER CITY***.

MARCHING ON TOGETHER

RIO FERDINAND'S £18 MILLION TRANSFER FROM *WEST HAM UNITED* TO *LEEDS UNITED* IN 2000 MADE HIM THE WORLD'S MOST EXPENSIVE DEFENDER. A YEAR LATER, *LILIAN THURAM'S* SWITCH FROM *PARMA* TO *JUVENTUS* SAW THAT RECORD ECLIPSED -- BUT THAT TRANSFER FEE WAS BLOWN OUT OF THE WATER BY THE £29.3 MILLION DEAL THAT TOOK *RIO* TO *UNITED* IN 2005.

IDENTIFY THESE OTHER REDS WITH *ELLAND ROAD* CONNECTIONS:

1 A TITLE WINNER WITH *LEEDS UNITED* IN 1992, HE WON LEAGUE TITLES WITH *UNITED* IN FOUR OF THE NEXT FIVE SEASONS.

2 *ENGLAND* WINGER WHO PLAYED FOR BOTH MANCHESTER CLUBS, *LEEDS, WEST BROMWICH ALBION, COVENTRY CITY* AND MORE.

3   WHEN *LEEDS* WERE RELEGATED IN 2004, THE CLUB COULD NO LONGER AFFORD HIS WAGES AND ENGINEERED HIS £7 MILLION MOVE TO *UNITED* RATHER THAN FACE ADMINISTRATION. AFTER THREE SEASONS AT *OLD TRAFFORD*, HE WENT ON TO PLAY FOR *NEWCASTLE UNITED*, *MK DONS* AND *NOTTS COUNTY*.

4   *SCOTLAND* INTERNATIONAL WINGER WHO HAD WON HONOURS WITH *ABERDEEN* AS A TEEN, HE WAS SOLD TO *UNITED* IN 1983 AFTER *LEEDS* FAILED TO EARN PROMOTION TO THE TOP FLIGHT.

5   AN FA CUP WINNER WITH *UNITED* IN 1963, HE BECAME A LEGEND AT *LEEDS*, WINNING LEAGUE, FA CUP AND LEAGUE CUP HONOURS IN HIS 12 YEARS AT *ELLAND ROAD*, DURING WHICH TIME HE BECAME PLAYER/MANAGER OF THE *REPUBLIC OF IRELAND*.

6   1991 PFA YOUNG PLAYER OF THE YEAR WHO WON MULTIPLE HONOURS AND *ENGLAND* RECOGNITION WITH *UNITED* BEFORE HIS CAREER TOOK HIM TO *LEEDS UNITED* AND FROM *SAMPDORIA* TO *BRADFORD CITY*.

7   *STOKE CITY* LEGEND WHO, LIKE HIS BROTHER *BRIAN*, PLAYED FOR BOTH *UNITED* AND *LEEDS*.

BABY-FACED ASSASSIN

OLE GUNNAR SOLSKJÆR WAS APPOINTED MANAGER OF **UNITED** IN 2018. BACK IN HIS PLAYING DAYS, THE NORWEGIAN INTERNATIONAL, WHOSE YOUTHFUL LOOKS EARNED HIM THE NICKNAME **"THE BABY-FACED ASSASSIN"**, SEEMED TO SPECIALISE IN COMING OFF THE BENCH TO SCORE VITAL GOALS FOR **UNITED** -- NONE MORE SO THAN THE SUPER-SUB'S EXTRA-TIME WINNER IN THE VICTORY OVER **BAYERN MUNICH** IN THE 1999 UEFA CHAMPIONS LEAGUE FINAL.

IDENTIFY THESE UNITED PLAYERS BY THEIR NICKNAMES:

1 *GOLDEN BALLS*

2 *PANCHO*

3 *LA BRUJITA (THE LITTLE WITCH)*

4 *SLABHEAD*

5 *THE GREAT DANE*

6 *THE GUV'NOR*

7 *EL APACHE*

8 *THREE LUNGS*

9 *SPARKY*

10 *MIKE*

CARLITO'S WAY

CARLOS TEVEZ JOINED **BOCA JUNIORS** AT THE AGE OF 16 AND MADE HIS DEBUT THE FOLLOWING YEAR. IN FOUR SEASONS WITH THE CLUB HE WON THE COPA SUDAMERICANA AND THE COPA LIBERTADORES, BEFORE JOINING BRAZIL'S **CORINTHIANS** FOR A RECORD £13.7 MILLION. HE CAPTAINED THEM TO THE LEAGUE TITLE IN 2005, WINNING HIS THIRD SOUTH AMERICAN FOOTBALLER OF THE YEAR AWARD IN THE PROCESS. IN 2006, **TEVEZ** AND FELLOW ARGENTINE **JAVIER MASCHERANO** LEFT **CORINTHIANS** FOR THE PREMIER LEAGUE AND **WEST HAM UNITED**. ALTHOUGH THE SIGNINGS SPARKED A LENGTHY DISPUTE REGARDING THIRD-PARTY OWNERSHIP OF PLAYING RIGHTS, **TEVEZ'S** GOALS WERE VITAL IN KEEPING **"THE HAMMERS"** IN THE TOP FLIGHT ... AND ENOUGH TO PERSUADE **UNITED** TO SIGN HIM ON A TWO-YEAR DEAL IN 2007. **TEVEZ** WON TWO LEAGUE TITLES, THE LEAGUE CUP, THE UEFA CHAMPIONS LEAGUE AND THE FIFA CLUB WORLD CUP WITH THE REDS -- BUT TRUE TO FORM, HIS TWO-YEAR TERM ENDED IN ACRIMONY. IN THE SUMMER OF 2009, HE JOINED **UNITED'S** TRADITIONAL FOES, **CITY**.

NAME THE TEAMS FROM WHICH **UNITED** SIGNED THESE ARGENTINES:

1 *ÁNGEL DI MARÍA*

2 *MARCOS ROJO*

3 *JUAN SEBASTIÁN VERÓN*

4 *GABRIEL HEINZE*

5 *SERGIO ROMERO*

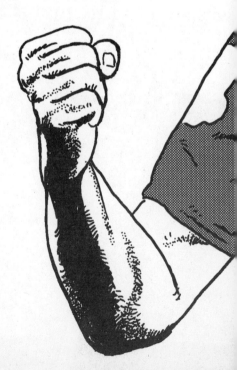

THE BOYS IN GREEN

ROY KEANE, PAUL MCGRATH AND *LIAM WHELAN* --
WHO WAS KILLED AT THE AGE OF 22 IN THE MUNICH AIR
DISASTER -- ARE THREE *REPUBLIC OF IRELAND*
INTERNATIONALS WITH *UNITED* CONNECTIONS WHO
HAVE BEEN FEATURED ON IRISH POSTAGE STAMPS.

NAME THESE OTHER *UNITED* PLAYERS WHO HAVE
REPRESENTED THE *REPUBLIC OF IRELAND:*

1   118 CAPS: THE *UNITED* PLAYER
WITH THE MOST *REPUBLIC*
CAPS, A DEFENDER WHO SPENT 12
SEASONS AT *OLD TRAFFORD* AND
SEVEN SEASONS WITH *SUNDERLAND*
BEFORE JOINING *READING* IN 2018.

2 59 CAPS: AFTER LEAVING **UNITED** IN 1963, HE SPENT THE BULK OF HIS PLAYING CAREER WITH **LEEDS UNITED** AND LATER MANAGED THE **REPUBLIC OF IRELAND** AS PLAYER/MANAGER IN THE 1970S.

3 56 CAPS: SIGNED TO **UNITED** FROM **OLDHAM ATHLETIC**, HIS HONOURS INCLUDED SEVEN PREMIER LEAGUE TITLES AND THE UEFA CHAMPIONS LEAGUE BEFORE LEAVING FOR **WOLVES** IN 2002.

4 36 CAPS: FULL-BACK SIGNED FROM **WEST HAM UNITED**, HE CAPTAINED **UNITED** IN THE 1963 FA CUP FINAL.

5 71 CAPS: **ARSENAL** AND **UNITED** STRIKER WHOSE 20 GOALS FOR HIS COUNTRY WAS A RECORD THAT STOOD FOR A DECADE.

6 71 CAPS: DEFENDER WHO REPRESENTED HIS COUNTRY AT FOOTBALL AND GAELIC FOOTBALL, HE WON TWO FA CUPS WITH **UNITED** IN THE MID-1980S BEFORE PLAYING FOR **SPORTING GIJON** AND **BLACKBURN ROVERS**.

7 8 CAPS: **UNITED'S** BACK-UP GOALKEEPER TO **ALEX STEPNEY** AND **GARY BAILEY**, LATER PLAYED FOR **BRENTFORD** AND **HALIFAX**.

8 33 CAPS: FULL-BACK WHO WON TWO LEAGUE TITLES, THE FA CUP AND THE EUROPEAN CUP WITH **UNITED**, HE LATER SPENT SIX YEARS WITH **BOLTON WANDERERS**.

THE BOYS OF 1968

A DECADE AFTER THE TRAGEDY
THAT DESTROYED A YOUNG
TEAM IN SEARCH OF EUROPEAN
GLORY, *UNITED* BECAME THE
FIRST ENGLISH WINNERS OF
THE EUROPEAN CUP

CAN YOU IDENTIFY THE MEMBERS OF THAT TRIUMPHANT TEAM BY THEIR SUBSEQUENT CAREER MOVES?

1 FOLLOWING A SHORT SPELL ON LOAN IN THE STATES WITH THE **MIAMI TOROS**, HE JOINED **PRESTON NORTH END** IN 1973.

2 HIE PLAYED A HANDFUL OF GAMES IN SOUTH AFRICA WITH **JEWISH GUILD** AFTER LEAVING **UNITED**, AND LATER PLAYED IN ENGLAND, IRELAND, SCOTLAND, AUSTRALIA, HONG KONG AND THE STATES.

3 JOINED **MIDDLESBROUGH** IN 1971 IN A £20,000 TRANSFER.

4 HE RETIRED FROM PLAYING IN 1971, WAS BRIEFLY ASSISTANT TO **TOMMY DOCHERTY** AND MANAGED **NORTHAMPTON TOWN**.

5 SUBSTITUTE WHO DIDN'T GET ON THE FIELD IN 1968 BUT WENT ON TO WIN THE EUROPEAN CUP WITH **ASTON VILLA**.

6 HE MOVED TO IRELAND IN 1970 TO BECOME PLAYER/MANAGER OF **WATERFORD UNITED**, WINNING TWO TITLES AND ADDING TO HIS TALLY OF 19 **REPUBLIC OF IRELAND** CAPS.

7 HE PLAYED FOR **ARSENAL, EVERTON, MANCHESTER CITY, BOLTON WANDERERS** AND TEAMS IN THE STATES BEFORE EMBARKING ON A MANAGEMENT AND COACHING CAREER.

8 HE SIGNED FOR **LUTON TOWN** IN 1972.

9 RETIRED IN 1970 AND SPENT FIVE YEARS AS **UNITED** YOUTH TEAM COACH BEFORE COACHING IN THE STATES, NORWAY AND JAPAN.

10 LEFT UNITED FOR **BOLTON WANDERERS** IN 1973, WHERE HE SPENT SIX YEARS AND HELPED THE CLUB WIN PROMOTION.

11 LEFT **UNITED** FOR **DALLAS TORNADO**, BEFORE RETIRING IN 1980, ALTHOUGH HE DID SUBSEQUENTLY TURN OUT FOR **ALTRINCHAM**.

12 HE LEFT **UNITED** TO BECOME MANAGER OF **PRESTON NORTH END** FOR THE 1973-74 SEASON.

BECKHAM'S BOSSES

IN A 20-YEAR PLAYING CAREER, *DAVID BECKHAM* WON 19 MAJOR TROPHIES, INCLUDING LEAGUE TITLES IN FOUR DIFFERENT COUNTRIES. HE ALSO REPRESENTED *ENGLAND* 115 TIMES. TEST YOUR KNOWLEDGE OF THE MANAGERS UNDER WHOM HE PLAYED:

1 *BECKHAM* WAS REUNITED WITH WHICH FORMER *UNITED* ASSISTANT MANAGER AT WHICH CLUB?

2 *BECKHAM* PLAYED UNDER WHICH MANAGER AT BOTH *REAL MADRID* AND *PARIS SAINT-GERMAIN?*

3 HE PLAYED UNDER WHICH MANAGER AT *REAL MADRID* AND FOR *ENGLAND?*

4 WHICH EUROPEAN CHAMPIONSHIP-WINNING PLAYER COACHED *BECKHAM* AT *LA GALAXY?*

5 AT WHICH CLUB DID *BECKHAM* PLAY UNDER *GARY PETERS?*

6 NAME THE *US SOCCER* TEAM'S LONGEST-SERVING HEAD COACH UNDER WHOM *BECKHAM* PLAYED AT *LA GALAXY.*

7 WHO WAS THE *ENGLAND* MANAGER WHO GAVE *BECKHAM* HIS INTERNATIONAL DEBUT IN 1996?

8 NAME THE FORMER *UNITED* ASSISTANT MANAGER WHO MANAGED *BECKHAM* IN THE *ENGLAND* TEAM.

9 WHO WAS THE MANAGER WHO GAVE *BECKHAM* HIS 115TH AND FINAL *ENGLAND* CAP IN 2009?

THE BOYS OF 2008

UNITED WERE CROWNED KINGS OF EUROPE FOR THE THIRD TIME WHEN THEY DEFEATED **CHELSEA** IN THE 2008 UEFA CHAMPIONS LEAGUE FINAL IN MOSCOW. WITH THE SCORES TIED AT 1-1, THE GAME WENT TO A PENALTY SHOOT-OUT. ALTHOUGH STAR **CRISTIANO RONALDO** MISSED HIS SPOT KICK, THE REDS PREVAILED WHEN **EDWIN VAN DER SAR** DENIED **CHELSEA'S NICOLAS ANELKA**.

WES BROWN, PAUL SCHOLES, JOHN O'SHEA, RYAN GIGGS AND **DARREN FLETCHER** WERE PRODUCTS OF THE UNITED YOUTH SYSTEM ... BUT CAN YOU NAME THE CLUBS FROM WHICH THE OTHER MEMBERS OF THE TRIUMPHANT 2008 TEAM WERE SIGNED TO **UNITED**:

1 *EDWIN VAN DER SAR*

2 *RIO FERDINAND*

3 *NEMANJA VIDIĆ*

4 *PATRICE EVRA*

5 *OWEN HARGREAVES*

6 *MICHAEL CARRICK*

7 *CRISTIANO RONALDO*

8 *WAYNE ROONEY*

9 *CARLOS TEVEZ*

10 *TOMASZ KUSZCZAK*

11 *MIKAËL SILVESTRE*

12 *ANDERSON*

13 *NANI*

FROM ECUADOR TO WIGAN

HAVING WON A SERIE A TITLE IN HIS NATIVE ECUADOR, *ANTONIO VALENCIA* MADE THE MOVE TO EUROPE TO PLAY FOR *VILLAREAL* IN 2005. A SUBSEQUENT LOAN MOVE TO *WIGAN ATHLETIC* WAS MADE PERMANENT IN EARLY 2008. HIS FORM WAS STRONG ENOUGH TO ATTRACT THE INTEREST OF *UNITED*, WHO SIGNED HIM IN THE SUMMER OF 2009. IN HIS TEN SEASONS AT *OLD TRAFFORD*, HE WON MULTIPLE HONOURS, INCLUDING TWO PREMIER LEAGUE TITLES AND THE UEFA EUROPA LEAGUE, AND ALONG THE WAY WAS CONVERTED FROM A FLYING WINGER TO A RIGHT-BACK. CAPPED 99 TIMES BY *ECUADOR*, HE RETURNED TO HIS NATIVE COUNTRY TO PLAY FOR *LDU QUITO*, BEFORE HANGING UP HIS BOOTS FOLLOWING A SEASON WITH MEXICO'S *QUERÉTARO*.

IDENTIFY THESE *UNITED* LINKS TO *WIGAN ATHLETIC*:

1 WHICH *UNITED* LEGEND BECAME A DIRECTOR OF *WIGAN ATHLETIC* AND STEPPED IN AS CARETAKER MANAGER OF THE TEAM IN 1983?

2 WHICH *NORTHERN IRELAND* INTERNATIONAL, CAPPED 86 TIMES BY HIS COUNTRY, WHO WENT ON TO PLAY FOR CLUBS INCLUDING *NEWCASTLE UNITED*, *LEICESTER CITY* AND *SHEFFIELD UNITED*, WAS LOANED OUT TO *WIGAN* BY BOTH *UNITED* AND *BLACKBURN ROVERS*?

3 A PREMIER LEAGUE WINNER WITH *UNITED* IN 2013, WHICH *ENGLAND* MIDFIELDER WAS LOANED OUT TO *LEICESTER CITY*, *WATFORD*, *WIGAN* AND *ASTON VILLA* BEFORE MAKING PERMANENT MOVES TO *EVERTON* IN 2015 AND *WATFORD* IN 2017?

4 SIGNED FROM *CREWE ALEXANDRA*, HE SCORED ON HIS *UNITED* DEBUT IN 2012 -- AGAINST *WIGAN ATHLETIC*. IN 2013, WHILE ON LOAN AT *WIGAN*, HE SCORED THE CLUB'S FIRST-EVER GOAL IN EUROPE. HE SUBSEQUENTLY JOINED ON A PERMANENT BASIS, WINNING THE EFL LEAGUE ONE TITLE IN 2018, BEFORE SIGNING FOR *STOKE CITY* IN 2019.

5 WHICH FORMER STALWART *UNITED* DEFENDER AND CAPTAIN HAS HAD TWO SPELLS MANAGING *WIGAN ATHLETIC*?

6 FORMER **UNITED, IPSWICH TOWN, WIGAN** AND **OLDHAM ATHLETIC** DEFENDER, HE WAS ANNOUNCED AS A FIRST-TEAM STRENGTH AND POWER COACH AT **UNITED** IN 2019.

7 **REPUBLIC OF IRELAND** DEFENDER WHO LEFT **UNITED** FOR **EVERTON** IN 2012, LATER PLAYED FOR **SUNDERLAND** AND **WIGAN ATHLETIC**, BEFORE SIGNING FOR **SALFORD CITY**.

8 **UNITED** CENTRE-HALF WHO, HAVING FOUGHT ON THE NORMANDY BEACHES IN THE D-DAY LANDINGS, WON THE FA CUP AND THE LEAGUE AND CAPTAINED THE REDS, PLAYED FOR AND MANAGED **GRIMSBY TOWN**, BEFORE MANAGING **WIGAN ATHLETIC** AND **HARTLEPOOL UNITED**.

HIS NAME IS RIO

LEEDS UNITED BROKE THE TRANSFER RECORD TO SIGN **RIO FERDINAND** IN 2000, AND **UNITED** SMASHED THAT RECORD TO LAND HIM TWO YEARS LATER. THE INVESTMENT WAS SHREWD -- HE WON SIX PREMIER LEAGUE TITLES, TWO LEAGUE CUPS, THE CHAMPIONS LEAGUE AND THE FIFA WORLD CUP IN HIS 12 SEASONS AT **OLD TRAFFORD**.

RIO WON HIS SIXTH LEAGUE TITLE IN 2013 BEFORE ENDING HIS CAREER WITH A SEASON AT **QUEENS PARK RANGERS**. WHICH CLUBS DID THESE MEMBERS OF THE 2012-13 TITLE-WINNING SQUAD SUBSEQUENTLY JOIN?

1 RAFAEL

2 PATRICE EVRA

3 JOHNNY EVANS

4 ANTONIO VALENCIA

5 ANDERSON

6 WAYNE ROONEY

7 CHRIS SMALLING

8 ANDERS LINDEGAARD

9 JAVIER HERNÁNDEZ

10 NEMANJA VIDIĆ

11 NANI

12 ASHLEY YOUNG

13 DANNY WELBECK

14 ROBIN VAN PERSIE

15 TOM CLEVERLEY

16 SHINJI KAGAWA

17 ALEXANDER
BÜTTNER

ROVERS AND RANGERS

THE FIRST MAN TO WIN PREMIER LEAGUE TITLES WITH TWO DIFFERENT CLUBS -- HE FOLLOWED UP HIS 1995 WIN WITH **BLACKBURN ROVERS** BY WINNING THE TITLE WITH **UNITED** IN 1999 AND 2000 -- **HENNING BERG** PLAYED 100 TIMES FOR **NORWAY**, SCORING NINE GOALS. HE RETURNED TO **BLACKBURN ROVERS** AFTER THREE SEASONS WITH **UNITED** AND ENDED HIS PLAYING DAYS WITH A SEASON AT **RANGERS**. IN 2005, HE EMBARKED ON THE MANAGEMENT CAREER THAT HAS TAKEN HIM TO NORWAY, POLAND, HUNGARY AND CYPRUS AND INCLUDES A DISASTROUS RETURN TO **BLACKBURN** WHICH ENDED IN HIS DISMISSAL AFTER 57 DAYS HAVING WON JUST ONE GAME IN HIS FIRST TEN.

IDENTIFY THESE OTHERS WHO HAVE PLAYED FOR **UNITED** AND **RANGERS:**

1   **ENGLAND** INTERNATIONAL MIDFIELDER WHOSE CLUBS INCLUDED **CHELSEA, UNITED, AC MILAN, PARIS SAINT-GERMAIN** AND **QUEENS PARK RANGERS**, HE WON A LEAGUE AND CUP DOUBLE WITH RANGERS IN 1989 AND A SECOND LEAGUE TITLE IN 1990.

2   FULL-BACK SIGNED FROM **PARTICK THISTLE** BY **TOMMY DOCHERTY**, HE WAS RELEGATED AND PROMOTED WITH **UNITED**, PLAYED IN THE 1976 FA CUP FINAL AND JOINED **RANGERS** IN 1979.

3   NICKNAMED **"THE GOALIE"** BY **RANGERS** FANS, HE WON BOTH THE SCOTTISH FOOTBALL WRITERS' AND SCOTTISH PROFESSIONAL FOOTBALLERS' ASSOCIATION PLAYER OF THE YEAR AWARDS, FIVE LEAGUE TITLES AND FIVE DOMESTIC CUPS DURING HIS TIME WITH **"THE GERS"**. HIS LENGTHY LIST OF OTHER CLUBS INCLUDED **OLDHAM ATHLETIC** AND **UNITED**.

4   ***UNITED*** ACADEMY GRADUATE WHO SPENT TIME ON LOAN AT A NUMBER OF CLUBS, INCLUDING ***RANGERS***, BEFORE PLAYING FOR ***SUNDERLAND*** AND ***STOKE CITY***, JOINING ***BURNLEY*** IN 2017.

5   IRISH INTERNATIONAL GOALKEEPER WHO WON HONOURS WITH ***UNITED***, ***WIGAN ATHLETIC***, ***LINFIELD*** AND ***OLYMPIACOS***, IN HIS SIX MONTHS AT ***RANGERS*** HE PLAYED IN JUST ONE GAME!

6   ***NORTHERN IRELAND*** MAINSTAY, HE WON THE 1977 FA CUP WITH UNITED, TWO LEAGUE TITLES AND MORE WITH ***RANGERS*** AND ENJOYED GREAT SUCCESS AS MANGER OF ***RAITH ROVERS***.

7   RUSSIAN WHO WON HONOURS WITH ***UNITED*** AND ***RANGERS***.

8   ***NORTHERN IRELAND'S*** ALL-TIME LEADING GOALSCORER.

PFA TEAM OF THE YEAR: 1974-1989

SINCE ITS INCEPTION IN THE 1973-74 SEASON, INCLUSION IN THE **PFA TEAM OF THE YEAR** IS CONSIDERED TO BE ONE OF THE HIGHEST ACCOLADES IN THE ENGLISH GAME, AS THE AWARD IS VOTED ON BY THE MEMBERS OF THE **PROFESSIONAL FOOTBALLERS' ASSOCIATION.** A SEPARATE TEAM FOR EACH OF THE FOUR DIVISIONS IS NAMED, AS WELL AS FEMALE FA WSL TEAM. ONE OF THE EARLIEST **UNITED** PLAYERS TO BE HONOURED WAS **FRANK STAPLETON** IN THE 1983-84 SEASON.

THE POSITIONS ARE DENOTED AS:
GK : GOALKEEPER   **DF : DEFENDER**
MF : MIDFIELDER   **FW : FORWARD**

NAME THE OTHER **UNITED** PLAYERS HONOURED BY THEIR PEERS:

1973-74: NO **UNITED** PLAYERS

1   1974-75 (SECOND DIVISION TEAM): **DF DF FW**

1975-76 AND 1976-77: NO **UNITED** PLAYERS

2   1977-78: **DF DF MF FW**

1978-79, 1979-80, 1980-81: NO **UNITED** PLAYERS

3   1981-82: **MF**

4   1982-83: **MF FW**

5   1983-84: **DF MF FW**

6   1984-85: **MF**

7   1985-86: **DF MF FW**

1986-87 AND 1987-88: NO **UNITED** PLAYERS

8   1988-89: **MF FW**

"THE DIVINE BALD ONE"

*LE DIVIN CHAUVE ("THE DIVINE BALD ONE"), 1998 WORLD CUP AND EURO 2000 WINNER **FABIEN BARTHEZ** ENDEARED HIMSELF TO **UNITED** FANS WITH HIS FLAMBOYANT AND ECCENTRIC DISPLAYS -- WHEN HE WASN'T GIVING THEM PALPITATIONS WITH HIS RISK-TAKING!*

***BARTHEZ** WON TWO PREMIER LEAGUE TITLES WITH **UNITED** IN HIS FOUR SEASONS AT THE CLUB BUT RETURNED TO FRANCE IN 2004 AFTER HE FELL OUT OF FAVOUR WITH MANAGER **SIR ALEX FERGUSON**.*

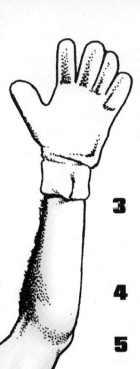

1 AFTER LAUNCHING HIS CARER AT **TOULOUSE**, **BARTHEZ** WON THE UEFA CHAMPIONS LEAGUE WITH WHICH CLUB IN 1993?

2 AGED 21, HE WAS THE YOUNGEST GOALKEEPER TO WIN THE UEFA CHAMPIONS LEAGUE UNTIL WHICH PLAYER IN 2000?

3 HE MOVED ON TO WHICH CLUB IN 2005, WINNING TWO LIGUE 1 TITLES AND PLAYING IN THE SIDE THAT ELIMINATED **UNITED** FROM THE CHAMPIONS LEAGUE IN 2008?

4 **BARTHEZ** WAS A WORLD CUP WINNER IN 1998 AS **FRANCE** DEFEATED WHICH NATION IN THE FINAL?

5 HE WAS A MEMBER OF THE **FRANCE** TEAM THAT DEFEATED WHICH COUNTRY IN THE EURO 2000 FINAL?

6 HE JOINED **UNITED** IN 2000, WHERE HE WAS LATER REUNITED WITH WHICH WORLD CUP-WINNING TEAMMATE?

7 IN A MEMORABLE MOMENT DURING A 2001 FA CUP FOURTH ROUND TIE AGAINST **WEST HAM UNITED**, **BARTHEZ** STOPPED PLAYING AND RAISED HIS HAND IN AN ATTEMPT TO **"PSYCH OUT"** WHICH ATTACKER INTO THINKING THAT OFFSIDE HAD BEEN CALLED -- THE RUSE FAILING WHEN THE ATTACKER WASN'T FOOLED AND CONTINUED ON TO SCORE THE WINNING GOAL?

8 THE ARRIVAL OF WHICH AMERICAN AT OLD TRAFFORD SIGNALLED THE END OF THE FRENCHMAN'S **OLD TRAFFORD** ADVENTURE?

9 AT THE HEIGHT OF HIS SUCCESS WITH THE **FRANCE** NATIONAL TEAM, **BARTHEZ** WAS IN A LONG-TERM RELATIONSHIP WITH WHICH CANADIAN SUPERMODEL?

10 NAME THE MANAGERS WHO STEERED **FRANCE** TO GLORY IN: A) THE 1998 WORLD CUP B) EURO 2000

YOUNG AND GIFTED

A PRODUCT OF **UNITED'S** YOUTH ACADEMY, THE 1992-93 **JIMMY MURPHY YOUNG PLAYER OF THE YEAR, PAUL SCHOLES** MADE HIS SENIOR DEBUT AT THE AGE OF 19 AND SPENT HIS ENTIRE PLAYING CAREER AT **OLD TRAFFORD.** HE MADE 718 APPEARANCES FOR THE CLUB AND HIS MEDAL HAUL INCLUDED 11 PREMIER LEAGUE TITLES, THREE FA CUPS, TWO UEFA CHAMPIONS LEAGUES, THE FIFA CLUB WORLD CUP AND MORE.

IDENTIFY THESE OTHER **JIMMY MURPHY YOUNG PLAYER OF THE YEAR** RECIPIENTS:

1 1989-90: SCORED THE ONLY GOAL IN THE 1990 FA CUP FINAL REPLAY AGAINST **CRYSTAL PALACE.**

2 1990-91 AND 1991-92: WENT ON TO WIN 13 PREMIER LEAGUE TITLES AND SERVE AS **UNITED** INTERIM AND ASSISTANT MANAGER.

3 1993-94: **INTER MIAMI'S** FIRST MANAGER.

4 1997-98 AND 1998-99: **ENGLAND** CENTRAL DEFENDER WHO SUBSEQUENTLY PLAYED FOR **SUNDERLAND, BLACKBURN ROVERS** AND **KERALA BLASTERS.**

5 1999-2000: BORN IN ILLINOIS, HE WENT ON TO PLAY FOR **WEST HAM UNITED** AND **BIRMINGHAM CITY** AND WAS CAPPED 36 TIMES BY THE **UNITED STATES.**

6 2001-02: BORN IN THE USA, CAPPED 30 TIMES BY **ITALY.**

7 2002-03: ITALIAN YOUNGSTER WHOSE SUBSEQUENT CLUBS INCLUDE **SAMPDORIA, CARDIFF CITY** AND **PANATHINAIKOS.**

8 2003-04: BORN IN THE DEMOCRATIC REPUBLIC OF CONGO, HE HAS REPRESENTED **ENGLAND** AT JUNIOR AND YOUTH LEVELS.

9 2004-05: **ENGLAND** INTERNATIONAL AWARDED THE MBE IN 2020.

10 2005-06: A 2019 EUROPA LEAGUE MATCH GOAL AGED 17 YEARS AND 353 DAYS MADE HIM **UNITED'S** YOUNGEST EUROPEAN SCORER.

TOP OF THE WORLD!

THE FINAL OF THE 2008 FIFA CLUB WORLD CUP, THE TOURNAMENT CONTESTED BY THE CHAMPION CLUBS FROM EACH OF FIFA'S SIX CONTINENTAL CONFEDERATIONS, PITTED **UNITED** AGAINST ECUADOR'S **LDU QUITO**. DESPITE GOING DOWN TO TEN MEN EARLY IN THE SECOND HALF WHEN **NEMANJA VIDIĆ** WAS RED-CARDED, A **WAYNE ROONEY** GOAL MADE THE REDS WORLD CHAMPIONS!

NAME THE CLUB TO WHICH EACH TEAM MEMBER WAS SUBSEQUENTLY SOLD, OR IF THEY RETIRED AFTER PLAYING FOR **UNITED**.

1 *EDWIN VAN DER SAR*

2 *RAFAEL*

3 *RIO FERDINAND*

4 *NEMANJA VIDIĆ*

5 *PATRICE EVRA*

6 *PARK JI-SUNG*

7 *MICHAEL CARRICK*

8 *ANDERSON*

9 *CRISTIANO RONALDO*

10 *CARLOS TEVEZ*

11 *WAYNE ROONEY*

12 *JONNY EVANS*

13 *GARY NEVILLE*

14 *DARREN FLETCHER*

2010 MEN!

A TWO-TIME WINNER OF BOTH THE PICHICHI TROPHY -- THE AWARD GIVEN TO THE TOP SCORER IN LA LIGA -- AND THE EUROPEAN GOLDEN SHOE, **DIEGO FORLÁN** WON CLUB HONOURS WITH **UNITED, VILLAREAL, ATLÉTICO MADRID, INTERNACIONAL, PEÑAROL** AND HONG KONG'S **KITCHEE**, AND THE 2011 COPA AMÉRICA WITH **URUGUAY**. HIS PERFORMANCES AT THE 2010 WORLD CUP HELPED INSPIRE HIS COUNTRY TO A THIRD-PLACE FINISH AND EARNED HIM THE GOLDEN BALL, AND HIS FIVE GOALS EARNED HIM THE GOLDEN BOOT.

IDENTIFY THESE PAST, PRESENT OR FUTURE **UNITED** PLAYERS WHO REPRESENTED THEIR COUNTRIES AT THE 2010 WORLD CUP.

1 WHICH PLAYER REGISTERED THREE ASSISTS FOR **GERMANY**?

2 NAME THE FIVE **ARGENTINA** PLAYERS WITH **UNITED** LINKS.

3 IN ADDITION TO **FORLÁN**, WHICH OTHER **UNITED** STRIKER WAS A MEMBER OF **URUGUAY'S** 2010 SQUAD?

4 NAME THE TWO **UNITED** PLAYERS IN THE **ENGLAND** SQUAD.

5 NAME THE TWO **UNITED** PLAYERS IN THE **UNITED STATES** SQUAD.

6 **NEMANJA VIDIĆ** WAS A MEMBER OF WHICH SQUAD?

7 WHICH **UNITED** STRIKER PLAYED FOR THE **NETHERLANDS**?

8 WHICH ONE OF THESE THREE PLAYERS DIDN'T SCORE FOR HIS RESPECTIVE COUNTRY:
A) **JAVIER HERNÁNDEZ** FOR **MEXICO**
B) **PARK JI-SUNG** FOR **SOUTH KOREA**
C) **ALEXIS SÁNCHEZ** FOR **CHILE**

9 WHICH FORMER **UNITED** PLAYER WAS A MEMBER OF **BRAZIL'S** SQUAD?

10 WHICH FORMER **UNITED** ASSISTANT MANAGER COACHED **CRISTIANO RONALDO** AND THE **PORTUGAL** TEAM?

MEET THE NEW BOSS, SAME AS THE OLD BOSS

JAVIER HERNÁNDEZ WON TWO PREMIER LEAGUE TITLES WITH ***UNITED*** AND HONOURS WITH ***GUADALAJARA, REAL MADRID*** AND ***SEVILLA.***

"CHICHARITO" -- THE FIRST MEXICAN PLAYER TO PLAY FOR ***UNITED*** -- PLAYED UNDER ***DAVID MOYES*** AT ***UNITED*** AND LATER ***WEST HAM UNITED.*** NAME THE MANAGER THE FOLLOWING PLAYED UNDER TWICE AND AND THE OTHER CLUB WHERE THEY WORKED TOGETHER,

1 *NEMANJA MATIĆ*

2 *MAROUANE FELLAINI*

3 *GORDON STRACHAN (PRE-UNITED)*

4 *GORDON STRACHAN (POST-UNITED)*

5 *BASTIAN SCHWEINSTEIGER*

6 *REMI MOSES*

7 *JUAN MATA*

8 *ADNAN JANUZAJ*

9 *BRYAN ROBSON*

10 *ROMELU LUKAKU*

THE BELFAST BOY

CAPPED 37 TIMES BY HIS COUNTRY, *GEORGE BEST* WAS DESCRIBED BY THE *IRISH FOOTBALL ASSOCIATION* AS THE *"GREATEST PLAYER TO EVER PULL ON THE GREEN SHIRT OF NORTHERN IRELAND"* -- DESPITE NEVER PLAYING IN A WORLD CUP OR EUROPEAN CHAMPIONSHIP.

IDENTIFY THESE *UNITED* PLAYERS CAPPED BY *NORTHERN IRELAND:*

1 67 CAPS: AN FA CUP WINNER WITH UNITED IN 1977, HE PLAYED FOR *QUEENS PARK RANGERS* AND *NEWCASTLE UNITED* AND LATER MANAGED *CARLISLE UNITED* AND *HARTLEPOOL UNITED.*

2 91 CAPS: WON THREE PREMIER LEAGUES, TWO LEAGUE CUPS AND THE UEFA CHAMPIONS LEAGUE WITH *UNITED*, PROMOTION WITH *SUNDERLAND* AND THE FA CUP WITH *LEICESTER CITY.*

3 12 CAPS: TWO-TIMES LEAGUE WINNER, HIS CAREER WAS CUT SHORT BY INJURIES SUSTAINED IN THE 1958 MUNICH AIR DISASTER.

4 91 CAPS: SENT OFF IN THE 1982 WORLD CUP WIN AGAINST *SPAIN*, HE WON THE 1988 LEAGUE CUP WITH *LUTON TOWN* AND THE 1991 EUROPEAN CUP WINNERS' CUP WITH *UNITED.*

5 73 CAPS: CANADIAN-BORN 1977 FA CUP WINNER WITH *UNITED*, HE WON MULTIPLE HONOURS WITH *RANGERS*, FOUND MANAGEMENT SUCCESS WITH *RAITH ROVERS* AND *COWDENBEATH*, AND WAS APPOINTED *NORTHERN IRELAND* ASSISTANT MANAGER IN 2020.

6 86 CAPS: WINGER WHO LAUNCHED HIS CAREER AT *UNITED* IN THE EARLY 1990S AND WHOSE LENGTHY LIST OF CLUBS INCLUDE *NEWCASTLE UNITED, BLACKBURN ROVERS, LEICESTER CITY, SHEFFIELD UNITED* AND *GLENTORAN.*

7 45 CAPS: GOALKEEPER WHO JOINED *UNITED* FROM *WIGAN ATHLETIC* IN 2001 AND WON PREMIER LEAGUE AND FA CUP MEDALS BEFORE PLAYING FOR A NUMBER OF CLUBS, FROM *WEST HAM UNITED* TO *OLIMPIACOS*, AND BEING NAMED DANISH GOALKEEPER OF THE YEAR DURING A SPELL WITH *ODENSE BK.*

8 88 CAPS: RELEGATED AND PROMOTED WITH UNITED BEFORE WINNING THE FA CUP IN 1977, HE SUBSEQUENTLY PLAYED FOR *STOKE CITY*, *MANCHESTER CITY* AND *BURY* AND HIS MANAGEMENT CAREER INCLUDED THREE YEARS AS BOSS OF *NORTHERN IRELAND*.

9 95 CAPS: *NORTHERN IRELAND'S* ALL-TIME LEADING GOALSCORER STARTED HIS CAREER AT *UNITED*, HAD LENGTHY SPELLS WITH *PRESTON NORTH END* AND *LEEDS UNITED* AND WON THE DOUBLE WITH *RANGERS*.

10 41 CAPS: MIDFIELDER WHO, AFTER THREE YEARS AT *UNITED*, JOINED *HUDDERSFIELD TOWN* IN 1963, WHERE HE CAPTAINED THE SIDE TO PROMOTION IN 1970. AFTER NINE YEARS IN YORKSHIRE, DURING WHICH TIME HE BECAME THE CLUB'S MOST-CAPPED PLAYER, HE MOVED ON TO *BURY*.

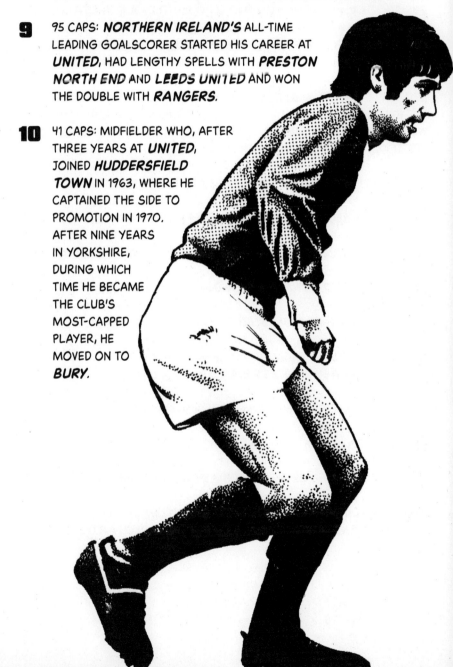

THE BUSBY BUYS

DAVID HERD MADE HIS NAME AT *ARSENAL*, JOINING *UNITED* IN A
£35,000 DEAL IN 1961. HE WON TWO LEAGUE TITLES AND THE FA CUP WITH
THE REDS AND WAS A SQUAD MEMBER WHEN *UNITED* WON THE EUROPEAN
CUP IN 1968. CAPPED FIVE TIMES BY *SCOTLAND*, HE LATER PLAYED FOR
STOKE CITY AND *WATERFORD* AND MANAGED *LINCOLN CITY*.

SIR MATT BUSBY WAS RENOWNED FOR BRINGING TALENT THROUGH
THE RANKS AT *UNITED* BUT, AS WITH HIS ACQUISITION OF *DAVID HERD*,
WOULD GO TO THE TRANSFER MARKET ON OCCASIONS TO STRENGTHEN
THE TEAM. IDENTIFY THESE OTHER *BUSBY* BUYS:

1 GOALKEEPER SIGNED FROM *CHELSEA* FOR £55,000 IN 1966.

2 BRITISH RECORD SIGNING FROM *SHEFFIELD WEDNESDAY* IN 1961.

3 BRITISH RECORD SIGNING FROM *TORINO* FOR £115,000 IN 1952.

4 *SCOTLAND* MIDFIELDER SIGNED FROM *CELTIC* IN 1962.

5 WINGER SIGNED FROM *BURNLEY* IN 1968.

6 WINGER SIGNED FROM *BIRMINGHAM CITY* IN 1951. HIS CAREER
WAS ENDED BY INJURIES RECEIVED IN THE MUNICH AIR CRASH.

7 GOALKEEPER SIGNED FROM *DARLINGTON* IN 1949.

8 IRISH FULL-BACK SIGNED FROM *WEST HAM UNITED* IN 1960.

9 IRISH GOALKEEPER SIGNED FROM *DONCASTER ROVERS* IN 1957.

10 CENTRE-FORWARD SIGNED FROM *BARNSLEY* IN 1953, AN
ENGLAND INTERNATIONAL KILLED IN THE MUNICH AIR DISASTER.

TOMMY DOC

ONE OF THE MOST COLOURFUL CHARACTERS THE BRITISH GAME HAS PRODUCED, **TOMMY DOCHERTY** LIKED TO JOKE THAT HE'D **"HAD MORE CLUBS THAN JACK NICKLAUS".** HE WAS REFERRING TO THE PROCESSION OF TEAMS THAT EMPLOYED HIS MANAGERIAL TALENTS FOLLOWING HIS SUCCESSFUL PLAYING CAREER.

1 AFTER LAUNCHING HIS PROFESSIONAL PLAYING CAREER AT **CELTIC** JUST AFTER THE SECOND WORLD WAR, HE JOINED WHICH ENGLISH TEAM IN 1949, WINNING THE SECOND DIVISION TITLE AND REACHING AN FA CUP FINAL DURING HIS NINE YEARS AT THE CLUB? (HE WOULD LATER SPEND A FEW MONTHS MANAGING THE CLUB AT THE TAIL END OF HIS COACHING CAREER.)

2 HE JOINED WHICH CLUB IN A £28,000 DEAL IN 1958?

3 IN 1961, HE ACCEPTED THE POSITION OF PLAYER/COACH AT WHICH CLUB, BECOMING MANAGER WHEN **TED DRAKE** LEFT IN 1962?

4 HIS SECOND JOB IN MANAGEMENT WAS AT **ROTHERHAM** -- **"I PROMISED I WOULD TAKE ROTHERHAM OUT OF THE SECOND DIVISION -- AND I TOOK THEM INTO THE THIRD"** -- AND HIS THIRD WAS AT **QUEENS PARK RANGERS**. NEITHER JOB LASTED LONG, NOR DID HIS NEXT POST, WORKING UNDER CHAIRMAN **DOUG ELLIS** AT WHICH CLUB?

5 IN THE EARLY 1970S, HE SPENT 18 MONTHS MANAGING WHICH EUROPEAN CLUB?

6 HE WAS REPLACED BY **WILLIE ORMOND** AS MANAGER OF WHICH TEAM WHEN HE LEFT TO TAKE UP THE **UNITED** JOB IN LATE 1972?

7 HAVING TAKEN **UNITED** DOWN A DIVISION AND THEN IMMEDIATELY TAKEN THEM UP AS CHAMPIONS, HAVING LOST AND WON FA CUP FINALS, A MARITAL SCANDAL SAW **DOCHERTY** SACKED BY **UNITED** IN 1977 AND REPLACED BY WHICH MANAGER?

8 HE THEN REPLACED **COLIN MURPHY** AS MANAGER AT WHICH CLUB?

9 WHICH CLUB SACKED HIM TWICE IN FIVE MONTHS IN 1980?

10 AFTER MANAGING TEAMS IN AUSTRALIA, IN 1984 HE TOOK THE REINS AT WHICH RECENTLY RELEGATED ENGLISH CLUB AND SUCCEEDED ONLY IN TAKING THEM DOWN ANOTHER DIVISION BEFORE BEING SACKED? *(IN FACT, THE SEASON AFTER HIS DISMISSAL, THE CLUB WAS RELEGATED YET AGAIN!)*

11 *DOCHERTY'S* LAST JOB IN MANAGEMENT WAS WITH WHICH NON-LEAGUE NORTHWEST CLUB, BEFORE HE RETIRED IN 1988?

THE DOC'S DISCARDS

ONE CASUALTY OF THE MANAGERIAL TURMOIL AT **UNITED** IN THE EARLY 1970S WAS **SCOTLAND** INTERNATIONAL **TED MACDOUGALL**. SIGNED BY **FRANK O'FARRELL**, HE ARRIVED AT **OLD TRAFFORD** IN SEPTEMBER OF 1972 WITH A REPUTATION AS A PROLIFIC GOALSCORER, BUT WITHIN THREE MONTHS, **O'FARRELL** WAS OUT. INCOMING BOSS **TOMMY DOCHERTY** DEEMED **MACDOUGALL** SURPLUS TO REQUIREMENTS AND BEFORE THE SEASON WAS OVER, HE WAS A **WEST HAM UNITED** PLAYER.

DOCHERTY MOVED A NUMBER OF PLAYERS OUT OF **UNITED** INCLUDING:

1 EUROPEAN CUP FINAL GOALSCORER SOLD TO **ARSENAL**.

2 ITALIAN-BORN, **UNITED'S** FIRST NON-BRITISH OR IRISH PLAYER.

3 PLAYED HIS FINAL GAME FOR UNITED ON APRIL 28, 1973 -- COINCIDENTALLY THE SAME DAY AS HIS BROTHER'S LAST APPEARANCE FOR **LEEDS UNITED**.

4 BOUGHT AND SOLD BY **TOMMY DOCHERTY** AFTER A LENGTHY CAREER WITH **SHEFFIELD WEDNESDAY** AND **WOLVES**, HE SET UP THE WINNING GOAL FOR **SOUTHAMPTON** IN THE 1976 FA CUP FINAL AGAINST HIS FORMER EMPLOYERS.

5 FORMER **ARSENAL** GREAT, AFTER TWO YEARS WITH **UNITED** HE WAS TRANSFERRED TO **PORTSMOUTH** IN 1974 -- HE SUBSEQUENTLY HAD A TROPHY-LADEN MANAGEMENT CAREER.

6 IMPOSING, AGGRESSIVE DEFENDER SIGNED BY **DOCHERTY**, HIS **UNITED** CAREER WAS DERAILED BY TWO BROKEN LEGS.

7 CLUB LEGEND RELEASED BY **DOCHERTY**, HE CAME BACK TO HAUNT **UNITED** WITH THE MOST FAMOUS BACKHEEL IN THE HISTORY OF DERBY GAMES.

THE DOC'S DEALS

STEVE COPPELL WAS PLAYING FOR **TRANMERE ROVERS** AND STUDYING ECONOMIC HISTORY AT LIVERPOOL UNIVERSITY WHEN **TOMMY DOCHERTY** SWOOPED IN TO SIGN HIM FOR **UNITED** IN A £60,000 TRANSFER DEAL IN 1975.

IDENTIFY THESE **UNITED** PLAYERS SIGNED BY **TOMMY DOCHERTY:**

1 A £70,000 BUY FROM **MILLWALL,** HE SCORED BOTH GOALS IN THE SEMI-FINAL THAT TOOK **UNITED** TO THE 1976 FA CUP FINAL AND PLAYED IN THE TEAM THAT WON THE TROPHY THE FOLLOWING YEAR. **DAVE SEXTON** SOLD HIM TO **DERBY** FOR £250,000 IN 1978.

2 SIGNED FROM **BRENTFORD** IN 1973, HE SPENT SEVEN YEARS AT **UNITED,** PLAYED FOR **SHEFFIELD UNITED** AND **COLCHESTER UNITED,** WAS ASSISTANT MANAGER AT **ARSENAL** AND MANAGED **QUEENS PARK RANGERS** IN THE MID-1990S.

3 STRIKER SIGNED FROM **HULL CITY,** CAPPED 15 TIMES BY **ENGLAND,** HE WON THE FA CUP WITH **UNITED** AND **WEST HAM UNITED.**

4 A MIDFIELDER CAPPED 51 TIMES BY THE **REPUBLIC OF IRELAND,** HE SPENT TWO YEARS AT **UNITED** BEFORE **JOHNNY GILES** SIGNED HIM TO **WEST BROMWICH ALBION.** HE LATER SPENT FIVE YEARS WITH **NEWCASTLE UNITED.**

5 A LEAGUE CUP AND INTER-CITIES FAIRS CUP WINNER WITH **LEEDS UNITED** AND A LEAGUE CUP WINNER WITH **STOKE CITY,** HE JOINED **UNITED** IN 1976, WHERE HE PLAYED ALONGSIDE HIS BROTHER.

6 SIGNED FROM **CELTIC** IN 1973, HE SPENT 11 YEARS AT **OLD TRAFFORD** AND PLAYED BRIEFLY AT **SWINDON TOWN** AS HE EMBARKED ON A SUCCESSFUL MANAGEMENT CAREER.

A BRACE FROM THE ACE

ONE OF THE MOST DECORATED FOOTBALLERS IN HISTORY, SWEDEN'S ALL-TIME TOP GOALSCORER **ZLATAN IBRAHIMOVIĆ** HAS WON HONOURS AT THE HIGHEST LEVEL IN THE NETHERLANDS, SPAIN, ITALY, FRANCE AND ENGLAND. HIS SOJOURN AT **UNITED** WAS BRIEF BUT PRODUCTIVE -- HE ARRIVED IN THE SUMMER OF 2016, WON THE FOOTBALL LEAGUE CUP AND EUROPA LEAGUE IN HIS FIRST SEASON AND WAS GONE TO TRY HIS LUCK IN THE MLS MIDWAY THROUGH HIS SECOND. HE SCORED **TWICE** IN **UNITED'S** 3-2 VICTORY OVER **SOUTHAMPTON** IN THAT 2017 LEAGUE CUP FINAL.

MORE RECENTLY KNOWN UNOFFICIALLY AS THE CARABAO CUP, THE EFL OR LEAGUE CUP HAS PREVIOUSLY BEEN COLLOQUIALLY KNOWN BY THE NAMES OF DIFFERENT SPONSORS OVER THE YEARS.

NAME **UNITED'S** OPPONENTS IN THESE LEAGUE CUP FINALS ... AND BONUS POINTS IF YOU RECALL THAT YEAR'S SPONSORS:

1 1983: A 1-2 LOSS

2 1991: A 0-1 LOSS

3 1992: A 1-0 WIN

4 1994: A 1-3 LOSS

5 2003: A 0-2 LOSS

6 2006: A 4-0 WIN

7 2009: WON IN A PENALTY SHOOT-OUT AFTER A 0-0 DRAW

8 2010: A 2-1 WIN

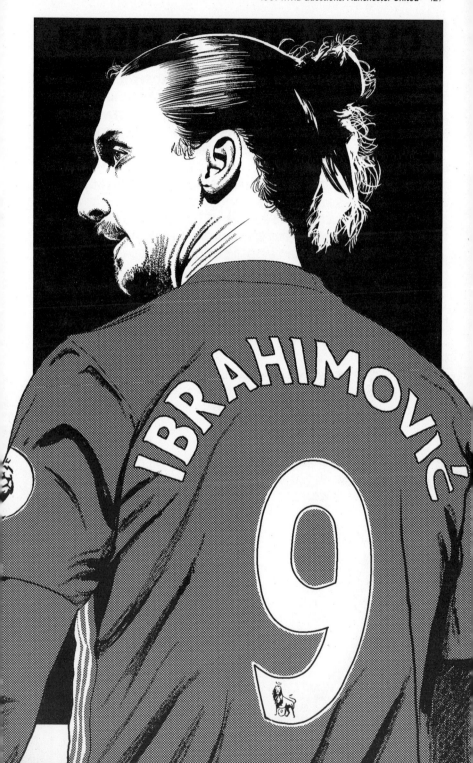

CLOSE BUT NO CIGAR

BASTIAN SCHWEINSTEIGER ABANDONED THE PROSPECT OF A CAREER IN PROFESSIONAL SKIING TO SIGN FOR **BAYERN MUNICH**. HE WON EIGHT BUNDESLIGA TITLES WITH THE BAVARIANS -- INCLUDING SEVEN LEAGUE AND CUP DOUBLES -- A UEFA CHAMPIONS LEAGUE, A FIFA CLUB WORLD CUP AND A UEFA SUPER CUP. A WORLD CUP WINNER WITH **GERMANY**, HE SPENT 18 MONTHS AT **UNITED**, WITH WHOM HE WON THE FA CUP AND THE EUROPA LEAGUE, BEFORE HEADING STATESIDE TO PLAY IN THE MLS.

ALTHOUGH HE HAD LEFT **UNITED** PRIOR TO THE EUROPA LEAGUE WIN, HE QUALIFIED FOR A MEDAL HAVING PLAYED IN EARLIER ROUNDS. IDENTIFY THESE **UNITED** PLAYERS WHO MISSED OUT ON MEDALS:

1   HAVING WON THE PREMIER LEAGUE EIGHT TIMES, HE RETIRED FROM THE GAME FOLLOWING A GAME AGAINST **WEST BROM** ON NEW YEAR'S DAY, 2011. WITH ONLY THREE LEAGUE APPEARANCES THAT SEASON, HE MISSED OUT ON A NINTH PREMIER LEAGUE MEDAL.

2   ALTHOUGH HE WAS WITH THE CLUB FOR FOUR SEASONS, THE HIGH-PROFILE SIGNING ONLY PICKED UP A WINNER'S MEDAL IN ONE OF THE THREE SEASONS THAT **UNITED** WON THE PREMIER LEAGUE DURING THAT TIME, HIS CAREER PLAGUED BY INJURIES. HE FARED NO BETTER AT HIS NEXT CLUB, CHALKING UP JUST ONE LEAGUE GAME IN THE 2011-12 SEASON AS THAT CLUB WON THE TITLE.

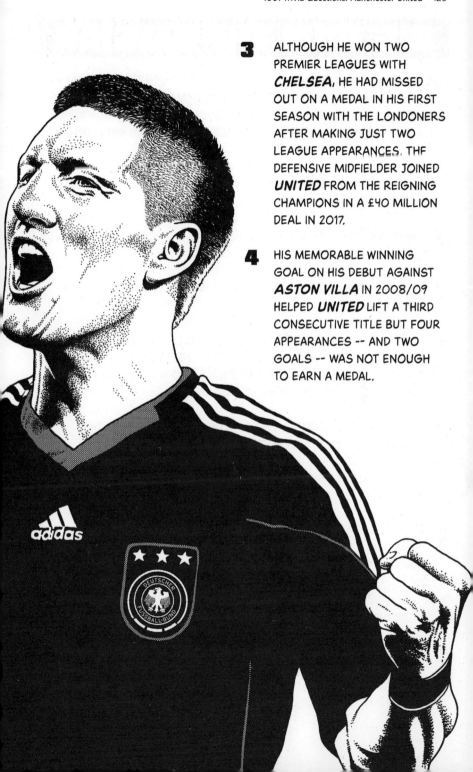

3 ALTHOUGH HE WON TWO PREMIER LEAGUES WITH *CHELSEA*, HE HAD MISSED OUT ON A MEDAL IN HIS FIRST SEASON WITH THE LONDONERS AFTER MAKING JUST TWO LEAGUE APPEARANCES. THE DEFENSIVE MIDFIELDER JOINED *UNITED* FROM THE REIGNING CHAMPIONS IN A £40 MILLION DEAL IN 2017.

4 HIS MEMORABLE WINNING GOAL ON HIS DEBUT AGAINST *ASTON VILLA* IN 2008/09 HELPED *UNITED* LIFT A THIRD CONSECUTIVE TITLE BUT FOUR APPEARANCES -- AND TWO GOALS -- WAS NOT ENOUGH TO EARN A MEDAL.

BIG ROM THE BELGIAN

SON OF A PROFESSIONAL FOOTBALLER WHO PLAYED IN BELGIUM AND WAS CAPPED BY *ZAIRE*, BELGIAN INTERNATIONAL *ROMELU LUKAKU* SPEAKS FLUENT FRENCH, DUTCH, ENGLISH, PORTUGUESE, ITALIAN, SPANISH AND A CONGOLESE SWAHILI DIALECT, AND CAN ALSO UNDERSTAND GERMAN!

1 HE TURNED PROFESSIONAL WITH WHICH CLUB, FINISHING TOP LEAGUE GOALSCORER -- AGED 16 -- WHEN THE CLUB WON THE BELGIAN PRO LEAGUE IN 2010?

2 WHO WAS THE MANAGER WHO SIGNED HIM TO *CHELSEA* IN AUGUST OF 2011?

3 THE FOLLOWING SUMMER, HE JOINED WHICH CLUB ON A SEASON-LONG LOAN?

4 LUKAKU JOINED *EVERTON* IN 2013, INITIALLY ON A SEASON-LONG LOAN DEAL THAT WAS FOLLOWED BY A £28 MILLION TRANSFER. WHO WAS HIS MANAGER AT *EVERTON*, WHO WOULD LATER MANAGE HIM WITH THE *BELGIUM* NATIONAL TEAM?

5 THE REPORTED £80 MILLION FEE AGREED BY *UNITED* TO TAKE *LUKAKU* TO *OLD TRAFFORD* WAS A CLUB RECORD FOR *EVERTON*, ECLIPSING THE £47.5 MILLION *CITY* PAID THEM FOR *JOHN STONES* AND THE £27.5 MILLION *UNITED* PAID FOR WHICH PLAYER IN 2013?

6 HE SCORED TEN GOALS IN HIS FIRST NINE APPEARANCES FOR *UNITED*, BREAKING THE RECORD OF NINE GOALS IN HIS FIRST NINE GAMES SET BY WHICH CLUB LEGEND SIX DECADES EARLIER?

7 HE JOINED *INTERNAZIONALE* IN 2019 -- WHO WAS THE FORMER *CHELSEA* MANAGER WHO SIGNED HIM TO THE ITALIAN GIANTS?

8 BELGIUM'S ALL-TIME LEADING GOALSCORER, HE WON THE BRONZE BOOT AT THE 2018 WORLD CUP. IN THAT TOURNAMENT, HE BECAME THE FIRST PLAYER SINCE WHICH SOUTH AMERICAN STAR IN 1986 TO SCORE TWO GOALS OR MORE IN CONSECUTIVE WORLD CUP GAMES?

VIVA ESPAÑA

RUUD VAN NISTELROOY WON LEAGUE TITLES IN THREE DIFFERENT COUNTRIES -- TWO EREDVISIE TITLES WITH *PSV EINDHOVEN* IN HIS NATIVE NETHERLANDS, THE PREMIER LEAGUE WITH *UNITED*, AND TWO LA LIGA TITLES IN SPAIN WITH *REAL MADRID*. HE WENT ON TO PLAY IN GERMANY WITH *HAMBURGER SV*, BEFORE ENDING HIS PLAYING DAYS BACK IN SPAIN WITH *MÁLAGA*.

WITH WHICH SPANISH CLUBS DID THE FOLLOWING PLAY?

1 *DAVID BECKHAM*

2 *MARK HUGHES*

3 *JAVIER HERNÁNDEZ*

4 *GABRIEL HEINZE*

5 *KEVIN MORAN*

6 *ÁNGEL DI MARÍA*

7 *JORDI CRUYFF*

8 *ASHLEY GRIMES*

9 *DIEGO FORLÁN*

10 *LAURIE CUNNINGHAM*

THE WEE MAN

GORDON STRACHAN BEGAN HIS CAREER AT **DUNDEE**, MAKING HIS SENIOR DEBUT IN 1974 AT THE AGE OF 17. HE WAS MADE CAPTAIN IN HIS SECOND SEASON BY NEW BOSS **ARCHIE GEMMILL**, BECOMING THE YOUNGEST CAPTAIN IN THE CLUB'S HISTORY. HE WAS THE FIRST PLAYER TO BE VOTED FOOTBALL WRITERS' PLAYER OF THE YEAR IN SCOTLAND AND ENGLAND. IN JULY OF 2019, AFTER PLAYING AND MANAGING AT THE HIGHEST LEVELS, HE RETURNED TO **DUNDEE** TO TAKE UP A POSITION AS TECHNICAL DIRECTOR.

1 HE SPENT SEVEN YEARS WITH **ABERDEEN**, THE MAJORITY OF WHICH TIME HE WAS MANAGED BY **ALEX FERGUSON** -- BUT WHO WAS THE MANAGER, A SUBSEQUENT **MANCHESTER CITY** AND **CELTIC** BOSS, WHO SIGNED **STRACHAN** TO THE CLUB?

2 HE WON TWO LEAGUE TITLES, TWO SCOTTISH CUPS AND THE 1983 EUROPEAN CUP WINNERS' CUP WITH **"THE DONS"** -- WHO DID **ABERDEEN** DEFEAT IN THAT EUROPEAN FINAL?

3 WHO WAS THE MANAGER WHO SIGNED HIM TO **UNITED** IN 1984?

4 WHICH MANAGER SIGNED **STRACHAN** TO **LEEDS UNITED** IN 1989?

5 HE WON PROMOTION AND THEN THE TOP FLIGHT TITLE WITH **LEEDS** BEFORE WHICH MANAGER SIGNED HIM AS PLAYER AND ASSISTANT MANAGER AT **COVENTRY CITY** IN 1995?

6 SUBSEQUENTLY APPOINTED MANAGER OF **COVENTRY**, HE WAS SACKED IN 2001, BUT APPOINTED AT WHICH CLUB WEEKS LATER?

7 HIS NEXT JOB IN MANAGEMENT WAS AT **CELTIC**, WHERE HE REPLACED WHICH MANAGER IN 2005?

8 AFTER HIS FOUR YEARS AT **CELTIC** YIELDED MULTIPLE DOMESTIC HONOURS, HE SPENT A YEAR MANAGING WHICH CLUB?

9 IN 2013, WHO DID HE SUCCEED AS MANAGER OF **SCOTLAND**?

BRUCEY!

DESPITE WINNING EVERY DOMESTIC HONOUR, THE EUROPEAN CUP WINNERS' CUP AND EUROPEAN SUPER CUP WITH **MANCHESTER UNITED**, **STEVE BRUCE** NEVER EARNED A FULL **ENGLAND** CAP. BORN IN CORBRIDGE, NORTHUMBERLAND, ON DECEMBER 31, 1960, HE WAS TURNED DOWN BY NUMEROUS PROFESSIONAL CLUBS -- INCLUDING HIS BELOVED **NEWCASTLE UNITED** -- AND WAS ON THE VERGE OF STARTING AS AN APPRENTICE PLUMBER ON THE **SWAN HUNTER** DOCKYARD WHEN HE WAS OFFERED A TRIAL AT **GILLINGHAM**. HE TRAVELLED DOWN TO KENT WITH ANOTHER **WALLSEND BOYS CLUB** YOUNGSTER -- **BRUCE** WAS OFFERED A PLACE BUT THE CLUB TURNED DOWN **PETER BEARDSLEY**! HIS MANAGEMENT CAREER SAW HIM TAKE CHARGE OF NINE CLUBS BEFORE BECOMING **NEWCASTLE UNITED** MANAGER.

1 HE WON THE FOOTBALL LEAGUE CUP AND THE SECOND DIVISION CHAMPIONSHIP WITH WHICH CLUB BEFORE JOINING **UNITED**?

2 WHICH FORMER **ENGLAND** INTERNATIONAL WAS THE MANAGER WHO SIGNED **BRUCE** TO **BIRMINGHAM CITY** IN 1996?

3 HIS FIRST JOB IN MANAGEMENT WAS PLAYER/MANAGER AT WHICH CLUB IN 1998?

4 WHICH CLUB HAS HE MANAGED TWICE?

5 WHICH CLUB DID HE TWICE STEER TO PROMOTION TO THE PREMIER LEAGUE?

6 NAME THE THREE CLUBS HE MANAGED BETWEEN LEAVING **SUNDERLAND** IN 2011 AND TAKING OVER AS **NEWCASTLE UNITED** MANAGER IN 2019.

FERGIE'S FINDS

WHEN *SIR ALEX FERGUSON* SIGNED *WAYNE ROONEY* FROM *EVERTON* IN 2004, THE £20 MILLION DEAL, WITH AN ADDITIONAL £7 MILLION IN CONTINGENCY PAYMENTS, WAS THE HIGHEST FEE EVER PAID FOR A TEENAGER. DURING HIS 21-YEARS REIGN AT OLD *TRAFFORD*, *FERGUSONS* OTHER SIGNINGS INCLUDED EXPENSIVE ACQUISITIONS LIKE *ROBIN VAN PERSIE, DIMITAR BERBATOV* AND *RIO FERDINAND.* IDENTIFY THESE OTHER, LESS HEADLINE-GRABBING *FERGIE* BUYS:

1 £1,300,000 FROM *SOUTHAMPTON*, SEPTEMBER 1989

2 £2,000,000 FROM *QUEENS PARK RANGERS*, AUGUST 1991

3 £1,000,000 FROM *CAMBRIDGE UNITED*, AUGUST 1992

4 £1,200,000 FROM *BEŞIKTAŞ*, JULY 1996

5 £1,500,000 FROM *BARCELONA*, AUGUST 1996

6 £3,500,000 FROM *TOTTENHAM HOTSPUR*, JUNE 1997

7 £4,900,000 FROM *VENEZIA*, AUGUST 1999

8 £12,825,000 FROM *FULHAM*, JANUARY 2004

9 £3,500,000 FROM *DALIAN SHIDE*, JANUARY 2004

10 £18,000,000 FROM *TOTTENHAM HOTSPUR*, JULY 2006

11 £17,000,000 FROM *BAYERN MUNICH*, JULY 2007

12 £4,000,000 FROM *WEST BROMWICH ALBION*, JULY 2007

13 £7,000,000 FROM *FK PARTIZAN*, JANUARY 2009

14 £10,000,000 FROM *FULHAM*, JANUARY 2010

15 £17,000,000 FROM *BLACKBURN ROVERS*, JUNE 2011

16 £15,000,000 FROM *CRYSTAL PALACE*, JANUARY 2013

THE PEOPLE'S CHOICE

AMONG THE HONOURS THAT **ROBIN VAN PERSIE** WON DURING HIS THREE SEASONS AT **OLD TRAFFORD** WAS THE 2012-13 **SIR MATT BUSBY PLAYER OF THE YEAR**, AN AWARD PRESENTED TO THE PLAYER OF THE SEASON AS CHOSEN BY **UNITED** FANS. IDENTIFY THESE OTHER WINNERS:

1 GOALKEEPER WHO, BETWEEN THE 2013-14 AND 2017-18 SEASONS, BECAME THE FIRST PERSON TO WIN THE AWARD FOUR TIMES.

2 **ARGENTINA** DEFENDER WHO, IN 2004-05, BECAME THE FIRST PERSON FROM OUTSIDE EUROPE TO WIN THE AWARD.

3 THE SECOND PORTUGUESE PLAYER TO WIN THE AWARD.

4 SCOTTISH FORWARD WHO WAS THE FIRST RECIPIENT OF THE AWARD WHEN IT WAS INAUGURATED IN 1987-88, HE WON AGAIN IN 1991-92.

5 IRISH MIDFIELDER WHO, WITH HIS WINS IN 1998-99 AND 1999-2000, BECAME THE FIRST PERSON TO WIN IN CONSECUTIVE YEARS.

6 IN 2010-11, HE BECAME THE FIRST NORTH AMERICAN WINNER.

7 FORMER SOUTHAMPTON FULL-BACK WHO WON IN 2018-19.

8 THE SECOND SPANISH PLAYER TO WIN THE AWARD, A MIDFIELDER WHOSE VICTORY CAME IN 2016-17.

9 THE SECOND SOUTH AMERICAN TO WIN, A WINGER WHOSE CONVERSION TO FULL-BACK HELPED EARN HIS 2011-12 AWARD.

10 THE FIRST DUTCH PLAYER TO WIN, HIS TWO VICTORIES CAME IN THE 2001-02 AND 2002-03 SEASONS.

11 1990-91 RECIPIENT, THE FIRST ACADEMY GRADUATE AND THE FIRST WELSH PLAYER TO WIN THE AWARD.

12 **ENGLAND** DEFENDER WHO HAD TWO SPELLS WITH **MIDDLESBROUGH**, HE WON THE AWARD IN 1989-90.

DEFINITELY A KEEPER

TIM HOWARD'S INDIVIDUAL HONOURS INCLUDE THE 2009 FIFA CONFEDERATIONS CUP GOLDEN GLOVE, MLS GOALKEEPER OF THE YEAR AND THREE CONCACAF MEN'S GOALKEEPER OF THE YEAR AWARDS. DURING HIS TIME WITH *UNITED* HE WON THE 2004 FA CUP AND 2006 LEAGUE CUP.

NAME THE *UNITED* GOALKEEPER IN THESE FINAL VICTORIES:

1 1909 FA CUP FINAL

2 1948 FA CUP FINAL

3 1963 FA CUP FINAL

4 1968 EUROPEAN CUP FINAL

5 1977 FA CUP FINAL

6 1983 FA CUP FINAL

7 1985 FA CUP FINAL

8 1990 FA CUP FINAL

9 1991 EUROPEAN CUP WINNERS' CUP FINAL

10 1991 EUROPEAN SUPER CUP FINAL

11 1992 LEAGUE CUP FINAL

12 1994 FA CUP FINAL

13 1996 FA CUP FINAL

14 1999 FA CUP FINAL

15 1999 UEFA CHAMPIONS LEAGUE FINAL

16 1999 INTERCONTINENTAL CUP

17 2008 UEFA CHAMPIONS LEAGUE FINAL

18 2008 FIFA CLUB WORLD CUP

19 2009 LEAGUE CUP FINAL

20 2010 LEAGUE CUP FINAL

21 2016 FA CUP FINAL

22 2017 LEAGUE CUP FINAL

23 2017 UEFA EUROPA LEAGUE FINAL

I'LL BE BACK!

SHINJI KAGAWA WAS SIGNED BY **CEREZO OSAKA** WHEN HE WAS 17. HE REPRESENTED **JAPAN** AT THE 2007 FIFA U-20 WORLD CUP IN CANADA, AND PLAYED FOR HIS COUNTRY AT THE 2008 OLYMPICS. HE MISSED OUT ON A PLACE IN THE SQUAD FOR THE 2010 WORLD CUP, BUT HE WAS OUTSTANDING AT THE 2011 AFC ASIAN CUP, ALTHOUGH A BROKEN METATARSAL DEPRIVED HIM OF A PLACE IN THE FINAL AND **JAPAN'S** EXTRA-TIME VICTORY OVER AUSTRALIA. THE INJURY CURTAILED HIS FIRST SEASON AT **BORUSSIA DORTMUND**, ALTHOUGH HIS PRE-INJURY TALLY OF EIGHT GOALS IN 18 APPEARANCES HELPED HIS CLUB WIN THE BUNDESLIGA TITLE. THE FOLLOWING SEASON, HIS SUPERB FORM HELPED **DORTMUND** WIN A GERMAN LEAGUE AND CUP DOUBLE. IN 2012, **KAGAWA** BECAME **UNITED'S** FIRST JAPANESE PLAYER. AFTER WINNING A PREMIER LEAGUE TITLE WITH THE REDS, HE REJOINED **BORUSSIA DORTMUND** IN 2014.

NAME THESE PLAYERS WHO RETURNED TO A PREVIOUS CLUB:

1 STRIKER WHO FOUND EUROPEAN GLORY WITH **UNITED** BEFORE RETURNING TO **TOTTENHAM HOTSPUR**, THE CLUB WITH WHOM HE HAD PREVIOUSLY WON THE PREMIER LEAGUE GOLDEN BOOT.

2 AFTER A DECADE AWAY FROM THE CLUB, DURING WHICH TIME HE WON THE PREMIER LEAGUE, THE FA CUP, THE LEAGUE CUP AND THE EUROPA LEAGUE WITH **UNITED** AND A SERIE A TITLE WITH **INTERNAZIONALE**, WHICH **ENGLAND** INTERNATIONAL REJOINED **ASTON VILLA** IN 2021?

3 WHICH STRIKER SPENT TWO SEASONS WITH **UNITED** IN THE EARLY 1980S BEFORE RETURNING TO THE CLUB WHERE HE HAD WON TWO EUROPEAN CUPS AND A LEAGUE CUP?

4 WHICH 1983 FA CUP WINNER WITH **UNITED** HAD WON THE CHAMPIONS LEAGUE WITH **AJAX** EARLY IN HIS CAREER AND RETURNED TO THE AMSTERDAM CLUB TO WIN THE 1987 UEFA CUP WINNERS' CUP?

5 WHICH STRIKER SPENT A TOTAL OF TEN SEASONS WITH **UNITED,** HIS TWO SPELLS INTERRUPTED BY A SEASON WITH **BARCELONA** AND A SEASON WITH **BAYERN MUNICH?**

6 AUSTRALIAN GOALKEEPER WHO HAD TWO SPELLS AT *UNITED*, EITHER SIDE OF EIGHT SEASONS WITH *ASTON VILLA*.

7 SERBIAN INTERNATIONAL WHO LEFT *CHELSEA* TO WIN A LEAGUE TITLE WITH *BENFICA*, RETURNED TO *CHELSEA* AND WON TWO PREMIER LEAGUES, THEN SIGNED FOR *UNITED* IN 2017.

8 STRIKER WHO WON LEAGUE TITLES IN THREE COUNTRIES, WHO BEGAN AND ENDED HIS CAREER AT *HÖGABORGS BK*.

9 GOALKEEPER WHO WON THE 1990 FA CUP WITH *UNITED*, PLAYED FOR *ASTON VILLA*, *COVENTRY CITY* AND *BIRMINGHAM CITY*, RETURNED TO *UNITED* FOR A SEASON AND THEN HAD TWO SPELLS AT *WEST HAM UNITED*.

10 STARTED AT *UNITED*, WON HONOURS WITH *BURNLEY*, KEPT GOAL FOR *ENGLAND* AND REJOINED THE REDS IN THE SUMMER OF 2021.

11 DEFENDER WHO WON A CHAMPIONS LEAGUE WITH *UNITED* THEN RETURNED TO *BARCELONA* TO WIN THREE MORE!

THE GOALGETTERS!

WAYNE ROONEY IS **UNITED'S** ALL-TIME RECORD GOALSCORER. WHEN HE BROKE **BOBBY CHARLTON'S** RECORD IN 2017, **ROONEY** BECAME THE FIRST PLAYER TO SCORE 250 GOALS FOR THE REDS. BY THE TIME HE LEFT FOR **EVERTON** A FEW WEEKS LATER, HE HAD SET THE BAR AT 253.

CHARLTON'S RECORD OF 249 GOALS HAD STOOD FOR 34 YEARS. NAME THESE PLAYERS WHO SCORED 100 GOALS OR MORE FOR *UNITED*:

1   237 GOALS (1962-1973): *SCOTLAND'S* TOP GOALSCORER

2   211 GOALS (1937-1954): SCORED TWICE IN 1948 FA CUP FINAL

3   179 GOALS (1953-1962): MUNICH CRASH SURVIVOR

4   179 GOALS (1963-1974): *"EL BEATLE"*

5   168 GOALS (1919-1933): *"GIVE IT TO JOE"* STAR BETWEEN THE WARS

6   168 GOALS (1990-2014): WON 13 PREMIER LEAGUE TITLES

7   163 GOALS (1980-1986, 1988-1995): PLAYED IN SPAIN AND GERMANY

8   155 GOALS (1993-2013): MANAGED *OLDHAM ATHLETIC* IN 2019

9   150 GOALS (2001-2006): 2003 PREMIER LEAGUE GOLDEN BOOT

10   148 GOALS (1936-1954): WON THE 1948 FA CUP AND 1952 LEAGUE

11   145 GOALS (1961-1968): SCORED TWICE IN THE 1963 FA CUP FINAL

12   131 GOALS (1953-1958): CENTRE-FORWARD KILLED IN MUNICH CRASH

13   127 GOALS (1987-1998): SCORED WINNER IN 1992 LEAGUE CUP FINAL

14   126 GOALS (1996-2007): MANAGED *MOLDE* AND *CARDIFF CITY*

15   121 GOALS(1995-2001): 1994 PREMIER LEAGUE GOLDEN BOOT

16   118 GOALS (2003-2009): 2008 PREMIER LEAGUE GOLDEN BOOT

17   101 GOALS (1906-1915): SCORED FIRST-EVER *OLD TRAFFORD* GOAL

18   100 GOALS (1906-1919): WON TWO LEAGUE TITLES AND FA CUP

19   100 GOALS (1893, 1895-1900): TWO SPELLS WITH *NEWTON HEATH*

GOLDEN GOALS

HAVING GRADUATED THROUGH THE YOUTH RANKS AT *UNITED*, FRENCH
MIDFIELDER *PAUL POGBA* BROKE INTO THE FIRST TEAM IN THE 2012-13
SEASON ... BUT DECLINED A NEW CONTRACT AND STARTED THE FOLLOWING
SEASON AS A *JUVENTUS* PLAYER. HAVING WON FOUR SERIE A TITLES,
INCLUDING TWO LEAGUE AND CUP DOUBLES, HE RETURNED TO *UNITED* IN
A RECORD £89 MILLION DEAL IN 2016 ... AND WON THE LEAGUE CUP AND
THE EUROPA LEAGUE IN HIS FIRST SEASON BACK WITH THE REDS.

POGBA WAS A GOALSCORER IN THE 2016-17 EUROPA LEAGUE FINAL,
ALONG WITH *HENRIKH MKHITARYAN*, AS *UNITED* BEAT *AJAX* 2-0.
NAME *UNITED'S* GOALSCORERS IN THESE EUROPEAN AND WORLD GAMES:

1 1967-68: EUROPEAN CUP FINAL, WON 4-1 V *BENFICA*

2 1968: INTERCONTINENTAL CUP, LOST 1-2 ON AGGREGATE TO
ESTUDIANTES DE LA PLATA

3 1990-91: EUROPEAN CUP WINNERS' CUP, WON 2-1 V *BARCELONA*

4 1991: EUROPEAN SUPER CUP, WON 1-0 V *RED STAR BELGRADE*

5 1998-99: UEFA CHAMPIONS LEAGUE, WON 2-1 V *BAYERN MUNICH*

6 1999: INTERCONTINENTAL CUP, WON 1-0 V *PALMEIRAS*

7 2007-08: UEFA CHAMPIONS LEAGUE 1-1 V *CHELSEA*,
WON ON PENALTIES

8 2008: EUROPEAN SUPER CUP,
LOST 1-2 TO *ZENIT SAINT PETERSBURG*

9 2008: FIFA CLUB WORLD CUP, WON 1-0 V *LDU QUITO*

10 2010-11: UEFA CHAMPIONS LEAGUE, LOST 1-3 TO *BARCELONA*

11 2017: EUROPEAN SUPER CUP, LOST 1-2 TO *REAL MADRID*

12 UEFA EUROPA LEAGUE 1-1 V *VILLARREAL*, LOST ON PENALTIES

YOUNG GUNS (GO FOR IT)

CREATED BY THE PROFESSIONAL FOOTBALLERS' ASSOCIATION, THE PFA PLAYERS' PLAYER OF THE YEAR AND THE PFA YOUNG PLAYER OF THE YEAR AWARDS WERE FIRST PRESENTED FOR THE 1973-74 SEASON. IN 2006-07, **CRISTIANO RONALDO** BECAME THE SECOND PLAYER TO WIN BOTH AWARDS IN ONE SEASON, FOLLOWING **ANDY GRAY** IN 1976-77. **GARETH BALE** BECAME THE THIRD IN 2012-13.

IDENTIFY THESE **UNITED**-LINKED PFA YOUNG PLAYERS OF THE YEAR:

1 1975-76: WINGER PLAYING FOR **MANCHESTER CITY** AT THAT TIME.

2 1984-85: WELSH INTERNATIONAL **UNITED** STRIKER.

3 1990-91: **UNITED** WINGER SIGNED FROM **TORQUAY UNITED**.

4 1991-92 AND 1992-93: **WALES** INTERNATIONAL WINGER WHO WOULD SPEND HIS ENTIRE PLAYING CAREER AT **OLD TRAFFORD**.

5 1993-94: PROLIFIC STRIKER PLAYING FOR **NEWCASTLE UNITED** AT THAT TIME.

6 1996-97: **UNITED** GREAT WHO WOULD PLAY IN SPAIN, ITALY, FRANCE AND THE UNITED STATES.

7 1997-98: **LIVERPOOL** PLAYER WHO WOULD WIN HIS ONLY PREMIER LEAGUE TITLE WITH **UNITED** MORE THAN A DECADE LATER.

8 2004-05 AND 2005-06: **UNITED** LEGEND SIGNED FROM **EVERTON**.

9 2008-09: WINGER PLAYING FOR **ASTON VILLA** AT THAT TIME.

LILYWHITE LINKS

DANNY WELBECK MARKED HIS PREMIER LEAGUE DEBUT WITH A GOAL. HAVING REPRESENTED **ENGLAND** AT EVERY YOUTH LEVEL FROM THE AGE OF 14 ONWARDS, HE WON HIS FIRST **ENGLAND** CAP IN 2011. HAVING WON THE PREMIER LEAGUE, TWO FOOTBALL LEAGUE CUPS AND THE FIFA CLUB WORLD CUP, HE JOINED **ARSENAL** IN 2014. EARLY IN HIS CAREER, HE SHARPENED HIS STRIKER SKILLS ON LOAN AT **PRESTON NORTH END**, WHEN HE WAS **DARREN FERGUSON'S** FIRST SIGNING AS MANAGER.

1 EARLY IN HIS CAREER, WHICH SUPERSTAR SPENT PART OF THE 1994-95 SEASON ON LOAN FROM **UNITED** AT **PRESTON NORTH END**, MEMORABLY SCORING A GOAL DIRECT FROM A CORNER?

2 NAME THE THREE **UNITED** MANAGERS WHO WERE **PRESTON NORTH END** PLAYERS.

3 WHICH THREE MEMBERS OF **UNITED'S** 1968 EUROPEAN CUP SIDE LATER PLAYED FOR **"THE LILYWHITES"**?

4 SCOTTISH LEFT-BACK WHO LEFT **UNITED** FOR **SOUTHAMPTON** IN 1972, BEFORE MAKING 314 APPEARANCES FOR **PRESTON**.

5 AFTER LEAVING **UNITED** IN 1972, HE ENDURED TWO RELEGATIONS WITH **HUDDERSFIELD TOWN**, SCORED FOR **NEWCASTLE UNITED** AGAINST **MANCHESTER CITY** IN THE 1976 LEAGUE CUP FINAL, PLAYED FOR **BOLTON WANDERERS**, AND THEN ENDED HIS PLAYING DAYS AT **DEEPDALE** WITH **PRESTON**.

PFA TEAM OF THE YEAR: 1990-1999

INCLUSION IN THE **PFA TEAM OF THE YEAR** IS CONSIDERED TO BE ONE OF THE HIGHEST ACCOLADES IN THE ENGLISH GAME, AS THE AWARD IS VOTED ON BY THE MEMBERS OF THE **PROFESSIONAL FOOTBALLERS' ASSOCIATIO**N. A SEPARATE TEAM FOR EACH OF THE FOUR DIVISIONS IS NAMED, AS WELL AS FEMALE FA WSL TEAM. IN 1992-93, **PETER SCHMEICHEL** WAS NAMED GOALKEEPER OF THE SEASON.

THE POSITIONS ARE DENOTED AS:
GK : GOALKEEPER   DF : DEFENDER
MF : MIDFIELDER   FW : FORWARD

NAME THE OTHER **UNITED** PLAYERS HONOURED BY THEIR PEERS:

1989-1990: NO **UNITED** PLAYERS

1   1990-91: **FW**

2   1991-92: **DF FW**

3   1992-93: **SCHMEICHEL** PLUS **DF MF MF**

4   1993-94: **DF DF MF FW**

5   1994-95: **DF MF**

6   1995-96: **DF**

7   1996-97: **DF MF MF**

8   1997-98: **DF DF MF MF MF**

9   1998-99: **DF DF DF MF FW**

MON CAPITAINE

WITH REGULAR CAPTAIN *STEVE BRUCE* SIDELINED DUE TO INJURY, *ERIC CANTONA* WORE THE ARMBAND FOR THE 1996 FA CUP FINAL. IN THE DYING MINUTES OF THE GAME, THE FRENCHMAN VOLLEYED IN THE ONLY GOAL OF THE GAME FROM THE EDGE OF THE BOX TO GIVE THE REDS VICTORY OVER *LIVERPOOL*. THE WIN MADE *UNITED* THE FIRST CLUB IN HISTORY TO WIN THE LEAGUE AND FA CUP DOUBLE TWICE AND *CANTONA* THE FIRST FA CUP-WINNING CAPTAIN FROM OUTSIDE THE BRITISH ISLES.

NAME THE *UNITED* GOALSCORERS IN THESE FA CUP FINAL WINS:

1 1909: 1-0 V *BRISTOL CITY*

2 1948: 4-2 V *BLACKPOOL*

3 1963: 3-1 V *LEICESTER CITY*

4 1977: 2-1 V *LIVERPOOL*

5 1983: 2-2 V *BRIGHTON & HOVE ALBION*
1983 REPLAY: 4-0

6 1985: 1-0 V *EVERTON*

7 1990: 3-3 V *CRYSTAL PALACE*
1990 REPLAY: 1-0

8 1994: 4-0 V *CHELSEA*

9 1999: 2-0 V *NEWCASTLE UNITED*

10 2004: 3-0 V *MILLWALL*

11 2016: 2-1 V *CRYSTAL PALACE*

ATKINSON ACQUISITIONS

AS A PLAYER, *RON ATKINSON* -- WHOSE NICKNAMES INCLUDED *"BIG RON"* AND *MR. BOJANGLES"* -- SET THE CLUB APPEARANCE RECORD FOR *OXFORD UNITED.* AS A MANAGER, HE WON TWO FA CUPS WITH *UNITED* AND FOOTBALL LEAGUE CUPS WITH *SHEFFIELD WEDNESDAY* AND *ASTON VILLA.* HIS MOST FAMOUS SIGNING FOR THE REDS WAS *BRYAN ROBSON,* A PLAYER HE HAD PREVIOUSLY MANAGED AT *WEST BROMWICH ALBION.* IDENTIFY THESE OTHER *ATKINSON* ACQUISITIONS:

1 ANOTHER WHO HAD PLAYED AT *WEST BROMWICH ALBION* UNDER *ATKINSON,* HE ARRIVED AT *UNITED* A MONTH BEFORE *BRYAN ROBSON.* HIS CAREER WAS BLIGHTED BY INJURIES AND HE WAS FORCED TO RETIRE AT 28, AFTER EIGHT YEARS AT *OLD TRAFFORD.*

2 AN FA CUP WINNER WITH *ARSENAL,* HE WON THE TROPHY TWICE MORE WITH *UNITED.* HIS 20 GOALS FOR THE *REPUBLIC OF IRELAND* WAS A RECORD THAT STOOD FOR A DECADE.

3 HAVING ESTABLISHED HIS GOALSCORING CREDENTIALS WITH *STOKE CITY,* HE WON TWO FA CUPS AND THE UEFA CUP WITH *TOTTENHAM HOTSPUR,* JOINING *UNITED* ON LOAN IN 1983-84. HE SUBSEQUENTLY CARVED OUT A TV CAREER AS A FOOTBALL PRESENTER AND PUNDIT.

4 CENTRAL DEFENDER SIGNED FROM *ST PATRICK'S ATHLETIC.*

5 HIS HONOURS WITH *ASTON VILLA* INCLUDED THE LEAGUE AND THE EUROPEAN CUP. HE SPENT FIVE YEARS AT *UNITED,* WON PROMOTION WITH *LEICESTER CITY,* HAD A SPELL AT *PORT VALE* AND FINISHED HIS PLAYING DAYS WINNING PROMOTION WITH *WALSALL.*

6 HE JOINED *UNITED* FROM *COVENTRY CITY,* AFTER LAUNCHING HIS CAREER WITH *TOTTENHAM HOTSPUR.* SURPLUS TO REQUIREMENTS AFTER *ATKINSON* LEFT THE CLUB, HE WAS SOLD TO *WIMBLEDON,* WITH WHOM HE WON THE FA CUP IN 1988.

7 ANOTHER WHO HAD FLOURISHED UNDER *ATKINSON* AT *WEST BROM,* HE JOINED *UNITED* ON LOAN FROM *REAL MADRID* IN 1983. HE WAS KILLED IN A 1989 CAR CRASH IN SPAIN, AGED 33.

8 HAVING FAILED TO MAKE THE GRADE AT *UNITED*, HE BECAME A LEGEND AT *NEWCASTLE UNITED*, WON HONOURS AT *LIVERPOOL* AFTER HIS RECORD-BREAKING TRANSFER, STARRED FOR *ENGLAND* AT THE 1990 WORLD CUP AND PLAYED FOR *EVERTON, BOLTON WANDERERS, MANCHESTER CITY* AND MORE.

RECORD BREAKERS!

GEORGE BEST ONCE SCORED SIX GOALS IN A SINGLE GAME! RETURNING FROM A LENGTHY SUSPENSION IN 1970, THE **NORTHERN IRELAND** ACE HIT THE DOUBLE HAT-TRICK IN **UNITED'S** 8-2 CRUSHING OF **NORTHAMPTON TOWN** IN THE FIFTH ROUND OF THE FA CUP. **BEST'S** FEAT EQUALLED THE **UNITED** RECORD SET BY **HAROLD HALSE** IN THE 1911 CHARITY SHIELD GAME AGAINST **SWINDON TOWN**. CONVERSELY, **BOBBY CHARLTON** SCORED JUST SIX GOALS IN THE ENTIRE 1972-73 SEASON AND FINISHED **UNITED'S** TOP LEAGUE GOALSCORER! AS IF TO PROVE THAT WAS NO DISMAL FLUKE, THE SAME TOTAL MADE **SAMMY MCILROY UNITED'S** TOP LEAGUE GOALSCORER THE NEXT SEASON!

IDENTIFY THE FOLLOWING **UNITED** RECORD BREAKERS:

1 WHO SCORED 46 GOALS IN ALL COMPETITIONS IN 1963-64?

2 WHO SCORED 32 GOALS IN THE LEAGUE IN THE 1959-60 SEASON?

3 WHO HIT 31 PREMIER LEAGUE GOALS IN THE 2007-08 SEASON?

4 WHICH PLAYER SCORED IN TEN CONSECUTIVE GAMES IN 2003?

5 WHO SCORED **UNITED'S** FASTEST GOAL, AFTER JUST 12 SECONDS OF A 1984 LEAGUE CUP GAME AGAINST **BURNLEY**?

6 COMING ON AS A SUBSTITUTE IN A 2012 GAME AGAINST **NORWICH CITY**, WHOSE APPEARANCE WAS LIMITED TO A RECORD 11 SECONDS?

7 AGED 16 YEARS AND 19 DAYS WHEN HE KEPT GOAL AGAINST **MANCHESTER CITY** IN THE 1956 CHARITY SHIELD, WHO BECAME **UNITED'S** YOUNGEST FIRST-TEAM PLAYER?

8 WHICH **ENGLAND** WINGER MADE 206 CONSECUTIVE LEAGUE APPEARANCES FOR **UNITED** BETWEEN EARLY 1977 AND LATE 1981?

9 WHO IS **UNITED'S** OLDEST-EVER FIRST-TEAM PLAYER, AGED 46 YEARS, 281 DAYS AGAINST **DERBY COUNTY** IN 1921?

10 WHO HIT FOUR GOALS IN 13 MINUTES V **NOTTINGHAM FOREST**, 1999?

RECORD MAKERS!

IN 1970, POP SINGER **DON FARNDON** -- WHO TWO YEARS EARLIER HAD HIT NO. 3 ON THE UK POP CHARTS WITH **"INDIAN RESERVATION"** -- RELEASED THE SINGLE **"BELFAST BOY"**, A TRIBUTE TO **UNITED** STAR **GEORGE BEST**. THE RECORD REACHED NO. 32 AND SPENT FIVE WEEKS ON THE HIT PARADE. FOLLOWING **BEST'S** DEATH IN 1977, THE SINGLE WAS RE-RELEASED, CLIMBING TO NO. 77 ON THE CHARTS.

WHAT DO YOU RECALL ABOUT THESE OTHER **UNITED** POP SONGS?

1   **"COME ON YOU REDS"**, A SINGLE BY **THE MANCHESTER UNITED FOOTBALL SQUAD** THAT TOPPED THE BRITISH POP CHARTS FOR TWO WEEKS IN 1994, WAS WRITTEN AND PRODUCED BY WHICH ROCK GROUP?

2   WHICH **UNITED** STAR TOOK THE SINGLE **"OUTSTANDING"** TO NO. 68 ON THE POP CHARTS IN 1999?

3   RELEASED FOR THE 1983 FA CUP FINAL, WHICH SINGLE GAVE **THE MANCHESTER UNITED FOOTBALL SQUAD** A NO. 13 HIT?

4   A NO. 6 HIT IN 1995, **"WE'RE GONNA DO IT AGAIN"** FEATURED WHICH RAPPER, WHO WAS SEEMINGLY NEVER HEARD FROM AGAIN?

5   IN 1996, **1300 DRUMS FEATURING UNJUSTIFIED ANCIENTS OF M.U.** APPEARED ON **"TOP OF THE POPS"** TO PERFORM THEIR NO. 11 HIT DEDICATED TO WHICH **UNITED** STAR?

6   WHICH **UNITED** AND **SCOTLAND** STAR RECORDED THE 1976 TRACK **"OLD TRAFFORD BLUES"**?

7   WHAT WAS THE TITLE OF THE **OASIS**-REMINISCENT SINGLE BY **THE 1999 MANCHESTER UNITED FOOTBALL SQUAD** THAT REACHED NO. 11 ON THE POP CHARTS?

8   WHO WAS THE CARIBBEAN ARTIST WHO TOOK THE PIONEERING FOOTBALL SONG **"MANCHESTER UNITED CALYPSO"** -- AN ODE TO THE **BUSBY BABES** -- ONTO THE POP CHARTS IN 1957?

THE ISLAND BOY

DWIGHT YORKE WAS DISCOVERED AS A 17-YEAR-OLD DURING AN **ASTON VILLA** TOUR OF THE WEST INDIES IN 1989. FOLLOWING A TRIAL WITH THE CLUB, HE WAS SIGNED ON PROFESSIONAL TERMS AND MADE HIS SENIOR DEBUT IN MARCH, 1990. FOR THE NEXT FEW YEARS HE WAS DEPLOYED AS A WINGER -- BUT WHEN HE WAS SWITCHED TO STRIKER, HE HIT 25 GOALS IN THE 1995-96 SEASON. HE JOINED **UNITED** IN A CONTROVERSIAL £12.6 MILLION DEAL IN 1998, AFTER IT WAS ALLEGED THAT HE HAD *"DOWNED TOOLS"* TO FORCE A MOVE OUT OF **VILLA PARK**.

1 **DWIGHT** PLAYED 72 TIMES FOR THE NATIONAL TEAM OF WHICH CARIBBEAN TWIN-ISLAND REPUBLIC, LATER ACCEPTING THE POST OF ASSISTANT MANAGER FOLLOWING THE END OF HIS PLAYING DAYS?

2 WHO WAS THE **ASTON VILLA** MANAGER WHO DISCOVERED HIM?

3 NAME THE **ASTON VILLA** MANAGER WHO RELUCTANTLY SOLD HIM.

4 IN HIS TREBLE-WINNING DEBUT SEASON WITH **UNITED** HE BECAME THE FIRST NON-EUROPEAN PLAYER TO WIN THE PREMIER LEAGUE GOLDEN BOOT, SHARING THE AWARD THAT YEAR WITH WHICH **LEEDS UNITED** PLAYER AND WHICH **LIVERPOOL** PLAYER?

5 HE JOINED WHICH CLUB IN 2002, WHERE HE WAS REUNITED WITH HIS FORMER UNITED STRIKE PARTNER **ANDY COLE**?

6 HE PLAYED THE 2004-05 SEASON FOR WHICH CLUB UNDER THE MANAGERSHIP OF FORMER **UNITED** GREAT **STEVE BRUCE**?

7 **DWIGHT** CAPTAINED WHICH AUSTRALIAN TEAM TO VICTORY IN THE INAUGURAL A-LEAGUE GRAND FINAL IN 2006?

8 AFTER LEADING HIS COUNTRY TO THE FIRST WORLD CUP IN ITS HISTORY IN 2006, HE SIGNED FOR **SUNDERLAND** TO PLAY UNDER WHICH FORMER **UNITED** TEAMMATE?

9 **DWIGHT** IS FAMOUSLY CLOSE FRIENDS WITH WHICH LEGENDARY **WEST INDIES** BATSMAN, SCORER OF THE FIRST QUINTUPLE-HUNDRED IN FIRST-CLASS CRICKET HISTORY?

10 **DWIGHT** HAS A CHILD WITH WHICH GLAMOUR MODEL, WRITER AND REALITY TV STAR?

UNLUCKY!

ALTHOUGH **ENGLAND** GOALKEEPER **BEN FOSTER** WAS ON THE BOOKS AT **UNITED** FOR FIVE YEARS, MUCH OF THAT TIME WAS SPENT ON LOAN AT **WATFORD** OR OUT OF CONTENTION AT **UNITED** THROUGH INJURY. HE WAS TRANSFERRED TO **BIRMINGHAM CITY** IN THE SUMMER OF 2010. **UNITED** FINISHED THE 2010-11 SEASON AS CHAMPIONS, WHILE THE LUCKLESS **FOSTER** WAS RELEGATED WITH THE BRUMMIES.

HOW MANY OF THE TEAMS RELEGATED THE SAME SEASON THAT **UNITED** WON THE PREMIER LEAGUE CAN YOU NAME?

1   1992-93

2   1993-94

3   1995-96

4   1996-97

5   1998-99

6   1999-2000

7   2000-01

8   2002-03

9   2006-07

10 2007-08

11 2008-09

12 2010-11

13 2012-13

OFF TO THE TOFFEES

A TEENAGE SENSATION FOR *EVERTON* AND *ENGLAND*, 18-YEAR-OLD *WAYNE ROONEY* JOINED *UNITED* IN 2005. IN 13 SEASONS AT *OLD TRAFFORD*, HE CEMENTED HIS PLACE IN *UNITED* LEGEND, SETTING MULTIPLE RECORDS AND WINNING A MULTITUDE OF HONOURS. HE RETURNED TO HIS BOYHOOD CLUB IN 2017 AND AFTER ONE SEASON BACK ON MERSEYSIDE, DURING WHICH HE SCORED HIS MILESTONE 200TH PREMIER LEAGUE GOAL, HEADED STATESIDE TO PLAY IN THE MLS.

IDENTIFY THESE OTHERS WHO LEFT *UNITED* TO PLAY FOR *EVERTON:*

1 FRENCH DEFENSIVE MIDFIELDER WHO JOINED *UNITED* IN 2015 AFTER SEVEN SEASONS WITH *SOUTHAMPTON*. A LACK OF PLAYING TIME SAW HIM MOVE TO *EVERTON* TWO YEARS LATER.

2 *UNITED STATES* GOALKEEPER WHO REPLACED *FABIEN BARTHEZ* AS FIRST CHOICE AT *UNITED*. THE ARRIVAL OF *EDWIN VAN DER SAR* PROMPTED HIS MOVE TO *EVERTON*, INITIALLY ON LOAN. HE SPENT TEN SEASONS WITH *"THE TOFFEES"* BEFORE HEADING BACK TO THE STATES IN 2016.

3 ONE OF *"FERGIE'S FLEDGLINGS"*, HE SPENT

EIGHT YEARS AT *EVERTON* AFTER WINNING SIX PREMIER LEAGUE
TITLES, THREE FA CUPS, THE UEFA CHAMPIONS LEAGUE AND MORE
WITH *UNITED*.

4 FRENCH STRIKER WHOSE
GOALS FIRED *FULHAM*
BACK INTO THE TOP
FLIGHT, HE SPENT FIVE
TROPHY-LADEN
SEASONS AT *UNITED*
BEFORE PLAYING
FOR *EVERTON*,
SUNDERLAND
AND *LAZIO*.

5 WELSH WINGER
WHO JOINED
UNITED FROM
WREXHAM IN
1978 BEFORE
GOING ON TO PLAY
FOR *EVERTON*,
CHELSEA, *LEEDS*
UNITED AND MORE,
INCLUDING TWO
NOTABLE SPELLS WITH
STOKE CITY.

6 RUSSIAN WINGER WHO
WON EVERY DOMESTIC
TROPHY WITH BOTH *UNITED* AND
RANGERS, HIS OTHER CLUBS
INCLUDE *EVERTON*, *FIORENTINA*
AND *MANCHESTER CITY*.

7 *UNITED*, *EVERTON*, *SUNDERLAND*
AND *WIGAN ATHLETIC* MIDFIELDER
WHO WAS AT THE CENTRE OF A LEGAL
TUG OF WAR BETWEEN THE FOOTBALL
ASSOCIATIONS OF *NORTHERN IRELAND* AND
THE *REPUBLIC OF IRELAND* IN 2006.

IMPORTED FROM FRANCE

CAPPED 90 TIMES BY **COLOMBIA**, **RADAMEL FALCAO** IS HIS COUNTRY'S ALL-TIME TOP GOALSCORER WITH 35 GOALS. HAVING WON HONOURS WITH **RIVER PLATE**, **PORTO** AND **ATLÉTICO MADRID**, HE JOINED **UNITED** ON LOAN FROM **MONACO** IN 2014. THE MOVE FAILED BADLY, AS DID A SUBSEQUENT LOAN TO **CHELSEA**. HE RETURNED TO PARENT CLUB **MONACO** ... AND WON THE 2017 LIGUE 1 TITLE, FINISHING AS THE CLUB'S TOP SCORER WITH 30 GOALS IN 43 APPEARANCES!

FROM WHICH FRENCH CLUBS DID THE FOLLOWING JOIN **UNITED**?

1 **GABRIEL HEINZE** (2004)

2 **FABIEN BARTHEZ** (2000)

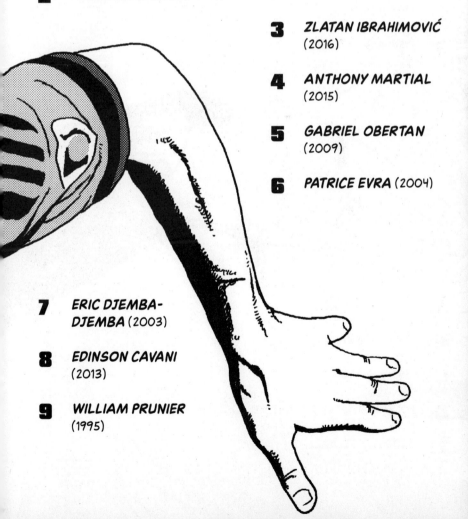

3 **ZLATAN IBRAHIMOVIĆ** (2016)

4 **ANTHONY MARTIAL** (2015)

5 **GABRIEL OBERTAN** (2009)

6 **PATRICE EVRA** (2004)

7 **ERIC DJEMBA-DJEMBA** (2003)

8 **EDINSON CAVANI** (2013)

9 **WILLIAM PRUNIER** (1995)

"SECOND MEANS NOTHING"

JOSÉ MOURINHO'S FIRST SEASON AT *UNITED* BROUGHT TRIUMPH IN
THE FOOTBALL LEAGUE CUP AND THE EUROPA LEAGUE ... AND ALTHOUGH
HIS SECOND SEASON STARTED WELL, *UNITED* FINISHED 19 POINTS BEHIND
CITY IN THE LEAGUE AND LOST THE 2018 FA CUP TO *CHELSEA* -- A TEAM
MOURINHO HAD MANAGED TWICE -- COURTESY OF AN *EDEN HAZARD*
PENALTY. *UNITED* STARTED THE NEXT SEASON BADLY AND BEFORE THE
END OF THE YEAR, *MOURINHO* WAS OUT.

WHO DEFEATED *UNITED* IN THESE FA CUP FINALS?

1   1957: A 1-2 LOSS

2   1958: A 0-2 LOSS

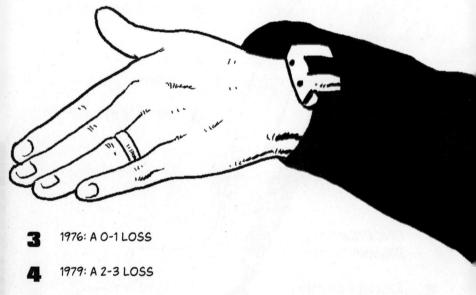

3   1976: A 0-1 LOSS

4   1979: A 2-3 LOSS

5   1995: A 0-1 LOSS

6   2005: 0-0 AFTER EXTRA TIME, LOST ON PENALTIES

7   2007: A 0-1 LOSS

STORMIN' NORMAN

A TEENAGE SENSATION FROM BELFAST, **NORMAN WHITESIDE'S** AGGRESSIVE AND PHYSICAL APPROACH TO THE GAME EARNED HIM THE NICKNAME **"THE SHANKHILL SKINHEAD"** FROM THE **OLD TRAFFORD** FAITHFUL. IN 1982, HE BECAME THE YOUNGEST PLAYER TO TAKE PART IN A FIFA WORLD CUP. HE WAS ALSO THE YOUNGEST PLAYER TO SCORE IN A LEAGUE CUP FINAL AND AN FA CUP FINAL -- BECOMING THE FIRST PLAYER TO SCORE IN BOTH FINALS IN THE SAME SEASON -- AND THE YOUNGEST PLAYER TO SCORE A SENIOR GOAL FOR **UNITED**.

1 **NORMAN** MADE HIS SENIOR DEBUT FOR **UNITED** TWO WEEKS BEFORE HIS 17TH BIRTHDAY IN 1982 -- WHO WAS THE **UNITED** MANAGER WHO SELECTED HIM?

2 HAVING PLAYED JUST TWO COMPETITIVE GAMES AT SENIOR LEVEL, HE WAS INCLUDED IN **NORTHERN IRELAND'S** 1982 WORLD CUP SQUAD BY WHICH MANAGER?

3 **NORTHERN IRELAND'S** OPENING GAME AGAINST **YUGOSLAVIA** WAS HIS INTERNATIONAL DEBUT. AT 17 YEARS AND 41 DAYS HE BROKE THE RECORD OF YOUNGEST-EVER WORLD CUP PLAYER SET BY WHICH TEEN AT THE 1958 WORLD CUP?

4 IN THE 1983 LOSS TO WHICH TEAM, HE BECAME THE YOUNGEST PLAYER TO SCORE IN A LEAGUE CUP FINAL?

5 THAT SAME SEASON, HE BECAME THE YOUNGEST PLAYER TO SCORE IN AN FA CUP FINAL WHEN HE NETTED IN THE 4-0 REPLAY WIN OVER WHICH TEAM?

6 TWO YEARS LATER, HE SCORED THE WINNING GOAL IN **UNITED'S** VICTORY OVER WHICH TEAM IN THE 1985 FA CUP FINAL?

7 **NORTHERN IRELAND** EARNED A SINGLE POINT AT THE 1986 WORLD CUP, **NORMAN** SCORING AGAINST WHICH NATION IN A 1-1 DRAW?

8 **WHITESIDE** JOINED WHICH CLUB IN 1989?

TURF MOOR TEEN IDOL

WILLIE MORGAN WAS *GEORGE BEST* BEFORE *GEORGE BEST!* THE *SCOTLAND* INTERNATIONAL WAS ONE OF THE FIRST PIN-UP PLAYERS, WITH HIS OWN FAN CLUB -- THE PRESIDENT WAS SUBSEQUENT POP STAR *DONOVAN* -- AND A CLOTHES BOUTIQUE CALLED *"SUPA-TEEK"*. WHEN HE FINALLY JOINED *UNITED* FROM *BURNLEY* IN 1968 HE TOOK THE NUMBER 7 SHIRT FROM *BEST!* AT THE HEIGHT OF HIS FAME THERE WAS EVEN A POP SONG BY *TRISTAR AIRBUS* -- *"WILLIE MORGAN ON THE WING"* -- PENNED BY *GRAHAM GOULDMAN* OF *10CC* FAME. AFTER SEVEN YEARS AT *OLD TRAFFORD* HE REJOINED *BURNLEY* IN 1975.

IDENTIFY THESE *UNITED* PLAYERS WITH *BURNLEY* CONNECTIONS:

1 WINGER WHO STARTED HIS CAREER AT UNITED BEFORE HELPING *BURNLEY* GAIN PROMOTION TO THE PREMIER LEAGUE IN 2009. HE SUBSEQUENTLY PLAYED FOR A NUMBER OF CLUBS, INCLUDING *BOLTON WANDERERS, BLACKPOOL, CHARLTON ATHLETIC, PORT VALE* AND *OLDHAM ATHLETIC.*

2 SCOTTISH INTERNATIONAL WHO WON CUP HONOURS WITH *ABERDEEN* AND *UNITED* AND MANAGED *BURNLEY* IN 1985.

3 AGGRESSIVE FULL-BACK WHO LEFT *UNITED* IN 2008, HAD SEVEN SEASONS WITH *SUNDERLAND* AND THREE WITH *STOKE CITY,* BEFORE JOINING *BURNLEY* IN 2017.

4 FORMER *BLACKBURN ROVERS* DEFENDER WHO WON NUMEROUS HONOURS IN HIS NINE YEARS WITH *UNITED,* BEFORE JOINING *BURNLEY* IN 2003.

5 MIDFIELDER WHO WON HONOURS WITH *BURNLEY, NORWICH CITY* AND *UNITED,* MANAGED *HULL CITY* AND WAS SUBSEQUENTLY APPOINTED ASSISTANT MANAGER TO *OLE GUNNAR SOLSKJÆR.*

6 PREMIER LEAGUE GOLDEN BOOT WINNER WITH *NEWCASTLE UNITED,* TREBLE WINNER WITH *UNITED,* HIS SUBSEQUENT CLUBS INCLUDE *BLACKBURN ROVERS, MANCHESTER CITY, BURNLEY, SUNDERLAND* AND *PORTSMOUTH.*

7 LEAGUE TITLE WINNER WITH *BURNLEY,* WORLD CUP WINNER WITH *ENGLAND,* HE WON A SECOND LEAGUE TITLE WITH *UNITED* IN 1965.

8 LOANED OUT BY UNITED TO *ROYAL ANTWERP, READING* AND *BURNLEY,* HE PLAYED FOR *WEST HAM UNITED* AND *STOKE CITY* BEFORE ESTABLISHING HIMSELF AS A FAN FAVOURITE AT *MILTON KEYNES DONS* BETWEEN 2008 AND 2014.

ENGLAND EXPECTS

DAVID BECKHAM MADE 115 APPEARANCES FOR **ENGLAND**, 59 OF THEM AS CAPTAIN. AS OF THE SUMMER OF 2021, TEN PLAYERS HAVE CAPTAINED **ENGLAND** WHILE ON THE BOOKS OF **UNITED**. IN ADDITION, PLAYERS SUCH AS THE **NEVILLE** BROTHERS AND **MICHAEL CARRICK** WERE HANDED THE CAPTAIN'S ARMBAND DURING A GAME, AND OTHERS, SUCH AS **MICHAEL OWEN** AND **PETER BEARDSLEY**, WERE NOT **UNITED** PLAYERS WHEN THEY LED OUT THE TEAM. **DAVID PLATT**, WHO CAPTAINED **ENGLAND** 19 TIMES, WAS ONLY WITH **UNITED** AS A YOUTH PLAYER.

NAME THE NINE OTHER **UNITED** PLAYERS WHO HAVE CAPTAINED **ENGLAND**.

THE GAFFERS

MATT BUSBY PLAYED EIGHT SEASONS WITH *MANCHESTER CITY*, DURING WHICH TIME HE WON THE 1934 FA CUP, BEFORE SIGNING FOR *LIVERPOOL* TWO YEARS LATER. HE CAPTAINED THE *ANFIELD* TEAM WITH DISTINCTION UNTIL HIS TOP-FLIGHT CAREER WAS EFFECTIVELY ENDED WITH THE OUTBREAK OF THE SECOND WORLD WAR.

IDENTIFY THESE *UNITED* MANAGERS BY THE TEAMS THE PLAYED FOR:

1 *SHETTLESTON, CELTIC, PRESTON NORTH END, ARSENAL, CHELSEA*

2 *ASTON VILLA, OXFORD UNITED*

3 *CLAUSENENGEN, MOLDE, MANCHESTER UNITED*

4 *CELTIC, CAMBRIDGE UNITED, BRISTOL CITY, SHREWSBURY TOWN, DUNFERMLINE ATHLETIC, HAMILTON ACADEMICAL, PRESTON NORTH END*

5 *RIO AVE, BELENENSES, SESIMBRA, COMÉRCIO E INDÚSTRIA*

6 *QUEEN'S PARK, ST JOHNSTONE, DUNFERMLINE ATHLETIC, RANGERS, FALKIRK, AYR UNITED*

7 *CORK UNITED, WEST HAM UNITED, PRESTON NORTH END, WEYMOUTH*

8 *NEWMARKET TOWN, CHELMSFORD CITY, LUTON TOWN, WEST HAM UNITED, LEYTON ORIENT, BRIGHTON & HOVE ALBION, CRYSTAL PALACE*

9 *AJAX, ROYAL ANTWERP, TELSTAR, SPARTA ROTTERDAM, AZ ALKMAAR*

DEEP IN THE FOREST

VIV ANDERSON SPENT THE FIRST TEN YEARS OF HIS PLAYING DAYS AT *NOTTINGHAM FOREST*, WHERE HE WON A SECOND DIVISION TITLE, THE FIRST DIVISION TITLE, TWO LEAGUE CUPS, TWO EUROPEAN CUPS AND THE EUROPEAN SUPER CUP, AS WELL AS LAUNCHING HIS *ENGLAND* CAREER. HAVING WON A LEAGUE CUP WITH *ARSENAL*, HE JOINED *UNITED* IN 1987 AND WON THE FA CUP THREE YEARS LATER.

IDENTIFY THESE OTHERS WHO PLAYED FOR *UNITED* AND *NOTTINGHAM FOREST*:

1 HAVING WON THE LEAGUE CUP WITH *NOTTINGHAM FOREST*, HE SPENT THREE YEARS WITH *UNITED*, DURING WHICH TIME HE WON BOTH DOMESTIC CUPS, THE EUROPEAN CUP WINNERS' CUP AND THE EUROPEAN SUPER CUP, BEFORE RETURNING TO *FOREST* IN 1992.

2 HAVING EXCELLED AS REGULAR TOP SCORER IN THE *FOREST* TEAM THAT INCLUDED *JOE BAKER* AND *ALAN HINTON* AND MADE A SERIOUS BID FOR LEAGUE AND FA CUP HONOURS IN THE MID-1960S, AN EXCITING WINGER WHO JOINED *UNITED* IN 1972 BUT WHOSE CAREER WAS SOON CURTAILED BY INJURY.

3 GOALKEEPER WHO COULDN'T GET A GAME FOR *UNITED* ON LOAN IN 1990 BUT WHO RETURNED TO *FOREST* TO RACK UP MORE THAN 300 APPEARANCES. HE LATER PLAYED FOR *MIDDLESBROUGH*, *FULHAM*, *OLDHAM ATHLETIC* AND OTHERS.

4 HE JOINED *UNITED* FROM *FOREST* IN 1993 FOR £3.75 MILLION, A BRITISH TRANSFER RECORD AT THE TIME.

5 SIGNED BY *RON ATKINSON* FROM *FOREST* IN 1986 AS THE INTENDED REPLACEMENT FOR *MARK HUGHES*, HE SPENT TWO YEARS AT OLD TRAFFORD UNTIL HE WAS SOLD TO *MIDDLESBROUGH* WHEN *HUGHES* RETURNED TO THE CLUB.

6 HAVING WON TWO EUROPEAN CUPS AND MORE WITH *NOTTINGHAM FOREST*, A STRIKER SIGNED WITH GREAT FANFARE TO *UNITED* FOR £1.25 MILLION IN 1980. THE MOVE DIDN'T PAN OUT AND HE WAS BACK AT *FOREST* THE FOLLOWING SEASON.

WORKING FOR THE MAN

ZLATAN IBRAHIMOVIĆ IS ONE OF THE MOST-DECORATED FOOTBALLERS IN THE HISTORY OF THE GAME. HE HAS PLAYED FOR SOME OF THE WORLD'S GREATEST TEAMS, UNDER SOME OF THE MOST SUCCESSFUL MANAGERS. TEST YOUR KNOWLEDGE OF **ZLATAN'S** BOSSES:

1 HE WAS REUNITED WITH **JOSÉ MOURINHO** AT **UNITED** AFTER WORKING WITH HIM AT WHICH OTHER CLUB?

2 AT WHICH CLUB DID HE PLAY UNDER **PEP GUARDIOLA**?

3 AT WHICH CLUB DID HE PLAY UNDER **ROBERTO MANCINI**?

4 AT WHICH CLUB DID HE PLAY UNDER **RONALD KOEMAN**?

5 AT WHICH CLUB DID HE PLAY UNDER **CARLO ANCELOTTI**?

6 WITH WHICH TEAM DID HE PLAY UNDER **DOMINIC KINNEAR**?

7 AT WHICH CLUB DID HE PLAY UNDER **LAURENT BLANC**?

8 AT WHICH CLUB DID HE PLAY UNDER **FABIO CAPELLO**?

PFA TEAM OF THE YEAR:
2000-2009

INCLUSION IN THE *PFA TEAM OF THE YEAR* IS CONSIDERED TO BE ONE OF THE HIGHEST ACCOLADES IN THE ENGLISH GAME, AS THE AWARD IS VOTED ON BY THE MEMBERS OF THE *PROFESSIONAL FOOTBALLERS' ASSOCIATIO*N. A SEPARATE TEAM FOR EACH OF THE FOUR DIVISIONS IS NAMED, AS WELL AS FEMALE FA WSL TEAM.
BETWEEN 2000 AND 2009, *RYAN GIGGS* WAS NAMED AS A MIDFIELDER FOUR TIMES.

THE POSITIONS ARE DENOTED AS:
GK : GOALKEEPER
DF : DEFENDER
MF : MIDFIELDER
FW : FORWARD

NAME THE OTHER *UNITED* PLAYERS HONOURED BY THEIR PEERS:

1   1999-2000: *DF MF MF FW*

2   2000-01: *GK DF DF MF GIGGS FW*

3   2001-02: *MF GIGGS FW*

4   2002-03: *MF*

5   2003-04: *GK FW*

6   2004-05: *DF DF*

7   2005-06: *MF FW*

8   2006-07: *GK DF DF DF DF MF MF GIGGS*

9   2007-08: *DF DF MF*

10   2008-09: *GK DF DF DF MF GIGGS*

BAFANARAMA!

QUINTON FORTUNE PLAYED 46 TIMES FOR **SOUTH AFRICA**, APPEARING AT THE 1998 AND 2002 WORLD CUPS. HE LAUNCHED HIS CAREER IN EUROPE AS A TEEN WITH **MALLORCA** AND **ATLÉTICO MADRID** BEFORE JOINING **UNITED** IN 1999. A PREMIER LEAGUE WINNER WITH THE REDS, HE LATER PLAYED FOR A NUMBER OF CLUBS, INCLUDING **BOLTON WANDERERS**, BEFORE EMBARKING ON A COACHING CAREER.

1 WHICH *UNITED* AND *ENGLAND* GOALKEEPER, HAVING BEEN RAISED IN SOUTH AFRICA, PLAYED FOR *KAIZER CHIEFS* IN THE LATE 1980S?

2 WHICH *CAMEROON* INTERNATIONAL REPRESENTED HIS COUNTRY AT THE 2002 WORLD CUP, WON THE FA CUP WITH *UNITED* IN 2004, AND PLAYED FOR CLUBS IN FRANCE, QATAR, DENMARK, ISRAEL, SERBIA, SCOTLAND, INDIA AND INDONESIA.

3 NAME THE *IVORY COAST* FORWARD WHO WAS THE LAST OF *SIR ALEX FERGUSON'S* SIGNINGS BUT FAILED TO ESTABLISH HIMSELF UNDER *DAVID MOYES* AND WAS LOANED OUT TO *CARDIFF CITY*.

4 SIGNED TO *UNITED* IN 2008 AND IMMEDIATELY LOANED OUT TO *PANATHINAIKOS*, WHO SCORED FOR *ANGOLA* AT THE 2008, 2010 AND 2012 AFRICAN CUP OF NATIONS AND PLAYED FOR CLUBS INCLUDING *HULL CITY*, *VALLADOLID* AND *RAYO VALLECANO*?

5 WHICH *SENEGAL* INTERNATIONAL WAS SIGNED TO *UNITED* IN 2009, LOANED OUT TO *MOLDE* AND PLAYED MOST OF HIS FOOTBALL IN ENGLAND WITH *BLACKBURN* AND *STOKE CITY*?

6 NAME THE *IVORY COAST* DEFENDER SIGNED TO *UNITED* FROM *VILLAREAL* IN 2016 IN A £30 MILLION DEAL.

7 NAME THE *NIGERIA* INTERNATIONAL, A FORMER *WATFORD* STRIKER, LOANED TO *UNITED* IN 2020 FROM CHINA'S *SHANGHAI GREENLAND SHENHUA*.

8 NAME THE *IVORY COAST* WINGER WHO JOINED *UNITED* FROM *ATALANTA* IN 2021.

IN HOT PURSUIT!

THE PREMIER LEAGUE IS THE MOST-WATCHED SPORTS LEAGUE IN THE WORLD, BROADCAST TO BILLIONS OF PEOPLE ACROSS 212 TERRITORIES. IT WAS INTRODUCED IN THE 1992-93 SEASON AND *UNITED* WERE THE FIRST WINNERS. THE CLUB WON THE TITLE IN 13 OF THE FIRST 21 SEASONS.

CAN YOU RECALL WHO THE RUNNERS-UP WERE IN THE 13 SEASONS THAT *UNITED* CLAIMED THE PREMIER LEAGUE TITLE?

1 1992-93: WON BY 10 POINTS

2 1993-94: WON BY 8 POINTS

3 1995-96: WON BY 4 POINTS

4 1996-97: WON BY 7 POINTS

5 1998-99: WON BY 1 POINT

6 1999-2000: WON BY 18 POINTS

7 2000-01: WON BY 10 POINTS

8 2002-03: WON BY 5 POINTS

9 2006-07: WON BY 6 POINTS

10 2007-08: WON BY 2 POINTS

11 2008-09: WON BY 4 POINTS

12 2010-11: WON BY 9 POINTS

13 2012-13: WON BY 11 POINTS

GOING FOR GOLD

20-YEAR-OLD *CARLOS TEVEZ* SCORED EIGHT GOALS IN SIX MATCHES, INCLUDING THE WINNER IN THE FINAL VICTORY OVER *PARAGUAY*, AS *ARGENTINA* ROMPED TO GOLD AT THE 2004 OLYMPIC GAMES. MANAGED BY *MARCELO BIELSA*, THE ARGENTINIANS SCORED 17 GOALS WITHOUT REPLY AS THE COUNTRY CLAIMED THE FIRST GOLD IN ANY OLYMPIC CATEGORY IN 52 YEARS! *TEVEZ* JOINED *UNITED* THREE YEARS LATER.

1 WHICH DEFENDER, WHO WAS A *UNITED* PLAYER AT THE TIME, WAS ALSO A MEMBER OF *ARGENTINA'S* 2004 GOLD MEDAL SQUAD, AND SCORED A GOAL AGAINST *SERBIA AND MONTENEGRO*?

2 WHICH *UNITED* PLAYER SCORED A GOAL FOR *PORTUGAL* AGAINST *MOROCCO* AT THE 2004 OLYMPICS?

3 WHICH TWO SUBSEQUENT *UNITED* PLAYERS REPRESENTED *ARGENTINA* AT THE 2008 OLYMPICS, ONE A GOALKEEPER AND THE OTHER THE SCORER OF TWO GOALS?

4 NAME THE THREE PLAYERS, ONE WHO WAS WITH *UNITED* AT THE TIME AND TWO WHO WOULD SIGN SUBSEQUENTLY, WHO WERE MEMBERS OF *SPAIN'S* SQUAD AT THE 2012 OLYMPICS.

5 WHICH FORMER *UNITED* PLAYER SCORED FOUR GOALS AT THE 2008 OLYMPICS TO WIN THE TOURNAMENT'S GOLDEN BOOT?

6 WHICH *UNITED* PLAYER SCORED A GOAL FOR *CHINA* AT THE 2008 OLYMPIC GAMES?

7 IN WHICH YEAR DID *UNITED'S HAROLD HARDMAN* WIN AN OLYMPIC GOLD MEDAL?

8 WHICH SUBSEQUENT *UNITED* PLAYER REPRESENTED THE *UNITED STATES* AT THE 2000 OLYMPIC GAMES?

9 WHICH *UNITED* PLAYER REPRESENTED *PORTUGAL* IN 2016?

10 WHICH ONE OF THE *PEREIRA DA SILVA* TWINS -- *RAFAEL* OR *FÁBIO* -- WAS A MEMBER OF *BRAZIL'S* 2012 OLYMPICS SQUAD?

YOU LITTLE RED DEVILS!

IN EARLY 1995, *ERIC CANTONA* WAS INVOLVED IN AN INCIDENT AT *CRYSTAL PALACE* THAT SAW HIM BANNED FOR EIGHT MONTHS -- AND FALL FOUL OF THE COURTS -- AFTER LAUNCHING A *"KUNG FU"* ATTACK ON AN ABUSIVE SPECTATOR.

SEE IF YOU CAN RECALL SOME OF THESE OTHER *UNITED* SCANDALS:

1 WHICH STAR RECEIVED AN EIGHT-MONTH BAN AND WAS FINED £50,000 IN 2003 FOR MISSING A SCHEDULED DRUGS TEST?

2 FOOTBALL WAS ROCKED IN 1915 BY A MATCH-FIXING SCANDAL INVOLVING *UNITED* AND WHICH OTHER CLUB, THAT RESULTED IN SEVEN PLAYERS BEING INITIALLY BANNED FOR LIFE?

3 DURING A DRESSING ROOM BUST-UP FOLLOWING AN FA CUP FIFTH ROUND DEFEAT TO *ARSENAL* IN 2003, WHICH PLAYER SUFFERED A GASHED EYEBROW WHEN AN IRATE *SIR ALEX FERGUSON* KICKED A BOOT IN HIS DIRECTION?

4 *"SO ROY KEANE'S ON 50 GRAND A WEEK. MIND YOU, I WAS ON 50 GRAND A WEEK UNTIL THE POLICE FOUND MY PRINTING MACHINE!"* WHICH FORMER *UNITED* PLAYER RECEIVED AN 18-MONTH PRISON SENTENCE IN 1993 FOR HIS INVOLVEMENT IN A COUNTERFEIT CURRENCY SCAM?

5 IN 2021, WHICH YOUNG *UNITED* AND *ENGLAND* STAR WAS SENT HOME, ALONG WITH *CITY'S PHIL FODEN*, FOR BREAKING COVID-19 QUARANTINE RULES WHILE ON INTERNATIONAL DUTY IN ICELAND?

6 WHICH *UNITED* PLAYER MADE HEADLINES IN 2011 WHEN HE WAS ALLEGED TO HAVE SHOPLIFTED A *KRISPY KREME* DOUGHNUT?

7 WHICH *UNITED* STAR WAS ARRESTED AND DETAINED AFTER AN ALTERCATION ON THE GREEK ISLAND OF MYKONOS IN 2020?

8 DUBBED *"THE BATTLE OF THE BUFFET"*, TEMPERS BOILED OVER IN THE TUNNEL AFTER A GAME IN 2004 AND, IN THE ENSUING BRAWL, *SIR ALEX FERGUSON* WAS STRUCK BY SLICE OF PIZZA THROWN BY *CESC FÀBREGAS*. WHO WERE *UNITED'S* OPPONENTS THAT DAY?

9 A DISPUTE OVER THE STUD RIGHTS OF WHICH RACEHORSE PROMPTED LEGAL ACTION BETWEEN *FERGUSON* AND *JOHN MAGNIER*, AT THAT TIME A MAJORITY *UNITED* SHAREHOLDER?

10 WHO HAD HIS £140,000 *BENTLEY* SEIZED BY POLICE IN 2009 AFTER IT WAS DISCOVERED HE DID NOT HAVE A FULL UK DRIVING LICENCE?

HEROES AND VILLAINS

RAISED IN A SERIES OF TOUGH ORPHANAGES, *PAUL MCGRATH* WORKED AS A SECURITY GUARD AND APPRENTICE METAL WORKER BEFORE TURNING PROFESSIONAL WITH *ST. PATRICK'S ATHLETIC*. AFTER SEVEN SEASONS WITH *UNITED*, DURING WHICH TIME HE WON THE 1985 FA CUP, HE JOINED *ASTON VILLA* IN 1989. IN EIGHT SEASONS IN THE MIDLANDS, *MCGRATH* -- WHO PLAYED 83 TIMES FOR THE *REPUBLIC OF IRELAND*, EARNING HERO STATUS FOR HIS WORLD CUP DISPLAYS -- WON THE FOOTBALL LEAGUE CUP AND WAS NAMED PFA PLAYERS' PLAYER OF THE YEAR.

IDENTIFY THESE OTHER REDS WITH *ASTON VILLA* CONNECTIONS:

1 NICKNAMED *"CANTONA"* AS A KID, A COMBATIVE CAMEROONIAN MIDFIELDER -- WHO UNITED FANS OPTIMISTICALLY DECLARED WAS *"SO GOOD THEY NAMED HIM TWICE"* -- HE JOINED *ASTON VILLA* IN 2005 AFTER 18 MONTHS AT *OLD TRAFFORD.*

2 VOTED OCEANIA GOALKEEPER OF THE CENTURY, AUSTRALIAN INTERNATIONAL WHO HAD TWO SPELLS WITH *UNITED*, WON TWO LEAGUE CUPS WITH *ASTON VILLA* AND WAS SACKED BY *CHELSEA* AFTER FAILING A DRUGS TEST.

3 HAVING PLAYED IN THE *ASTON VILLA* TEAM THAT BEAT *UNITED* IN THE 1957 FA CUP FINAL, HE SIGNED FOR THE REDS IN THE WAKE OF THE MUNICH AIR DISASTER AND WAS GIVEN SPECIAL DISPENSATION, ALTHOUGH TECHNICALLY CUP-TIED, TO PLAY IN THE *UNITED* TEAM THAT REACHED THE FA CUP FINAL IN 1958. LATER THAT SAME YEAR HE MOVED ON TO *CHELSEA.*

4 A PROMOTION WINNER WITH *WATFORD* IN 2006, HE WAS NAMED PFA YOUNG PLAYER OF THE YEAR WITH *ASTON VILLA.* AN *ENGLAND* INTERNATIONAL, HE JOINED *UNITED* IN 2011, WHERE HE WON FIVE TROPHIES -- INCLUDING THE PREMIER LEAGUE, THE FA CUP AND THE EUROPA LEAGUE -- BEFORE FOLLOWING A SUCCESSFUL SEASON IN SERIE A BY REJOINING *ASTON VILLA* IN 2021.

5 DEFENDER WHO WAS LOANED OUT BY *UNITED* TO *ROYAL ANTWERP, BURNLEY, RANGERS, ASTON VILLA* AND *SHEFFIELD UNITED*, BEFORE GOING ON TO PLAY FOR *SUNDERLAND, STOKE CITY* AND *BURNLEY.*

6 BORN IN THE DEMOCRATIC REPUBLIC OF CONGO, DEFENDER WHO SPENT TWO SPELLS ON LOAN WITH *ASTON VILLA* BEFORE, IN 2019, BECOMING THE YOUNGEST PLAYER TO CAPTAIN *UNITED* SINCE *NORMAN WHITESIDE* IN 1985.

7 ATTACKING LEFT-BACK, IN SEVEN YEARS WITH *ASTON VILLA* HE WON THE LEAGUE, THE EUROPEAN CUP AND THE EUROPEAN SUPER CUP BEFORE JOINING *UNITED* IN 1985.

8 NORWEGIAN DEFENDER WHO WON MULTIPLE HONOURS WITH *UNITED* BEFORE JOINING *ASTON VILLA* ON A FREE TRANSFER IN 2002.

PFA TEAM OF THE YEAR: 2010-2021

INCLUSION IN THE **PFA TEAM OF THE YEAR** IS CONSIDERED TO BE ONE OF THE HIGHEST ACCOLADES IN THE ENGLISH GAME AS THE AWARD IS VOTED ON BY THE MEMBERS OF THE **PROFESSIONAL FOOTBALLERS' ASSOCIATIO**N. A SEPARATE TEAM FOR EACH OF THE FOUR DIVISIONS IS NAMED, AS WELL AS FEMALE FA WSL TEAM. BETWEEN 2010 AND 2021, **DAVID DE GEA** WAS NAMED PREMIER LEAGUE GOALKEEPER FIVE TIMES.

THE POSITIONS ARE DENOTED AS:
**GK : GOALKEEPER   DF : DEFENDER
MF : MIDFIELDER   FW : FORWARD**

NAME THE OTHER **UNITED** PLAYERS HONOURED BY THEIR PEERS:

1   2009-10: **DF MF MF FW**

2   2010-11: **GK DF MF FW**

3   2011-12: **FW**

4   2012-13: **DE GEA** PLUS **DF MF FW**

2013-14: NO **UNITED** PLAYERS

5   2014-15: **DE GEA**

6   2015-16: **DE GEA**

7   2016-17: **DE GEA**

8   2017-18: **DE GEA**

9   2018-19: **MF**

2019-20: NO **UNITED** PLAYERS

10   2020-21: **DF MF**

GOLDEN BOYS

THE PREMIER LEAGUE GOLDEN BOOT IS AWARDED TO THE TOP PREMIER LEAGUE GOALSCORER EACH SEASON. *CRISTIANO RONALDO* WON THE AWARD PLAYING FOR *UNITED* IN THE 2007-08 SEASON, HIS 31 GOALS ALSO EARNING HIM THE EUROPEAN GOLDEN SHOE, THE AWARD GIVEN TO THE LEADING GOALSCORER ACROSS ALL THE TOP EUROPEAN LEAGUES.

IDENTIFY THESE *UNITED*-LINKED PREMIER LEAGUE GOLDEN BOOT WINNERS:

1 1992-93: 22 GOALS FOR *TOTTENHAM HOTSPUR*.

2 1993-94: 34 GOALS FOR *NEWCASTLE UNITED*.

3 1997-98: THREE-WAY TIE ON 18 GOALS INCLUDING TWO *UNITED*-LINKED PLAYERS -- ONE PLAYING FOR *COVENTRY CITY*, THE OTHER PLAYING FOR *LIVERPOOL*.

4 1998-99: THREE-WAY TIE ON 18 GOALS INCLUDING TWO *UNITED*-LINKED PLAYERS -- ONE PLAYING FOR *UNITED*, THE OTHER PLAYING FOR *LIVERPOOL* AT THAT TIME.

5 2002-03: 25 GOALS FOR *UNITED'S* DUTCH STRIKER.

6 2010-11: A TIE ON 20 GOALS BETWEEN A BULGARIAN PLAYING FOR *UNITED* AND A FORMER *UNITED* STAR PLAYING AT THAT TIME FOR *MANCHESTER CITY*.

7 2011-12: 30 GOALS FOR AN *ARSENAL* STRIKER.

8 2012-13: 26 GOALS FOR A DUTCH STRIKER PLAYING FOR *UNITED*.

WELL, I NEVER ...

WHEN HE WASN'T WINNING WORLD CUPS AND EUROPEAN CUPS, *BOBBY CHARLTON'S* EXTRACURRICULAR ACTIVITIES INCLUDED OWNING A TRAVEL AGENCY AND ESTABLISHING THE CHAIN OF WORLDWIDE SOCCER SCHOOLS THAT DISCOVERED *DAVID BECKHAM.*

WHICH *MANCHESTER UNITED* PLAYER:

1 EARNED A TAEKWONDO BLACK BELT AND SERIOUSLY CONSIDERED ABANDONING FOOTBALL TO WORK AS A DOCKER?

2 INVENTED A MUSICAL PERCUSSION INSTRUMENT CALLED *"THE DUBE"?*

3 WAS THE FIRST PERSON TO PLAY IN A FIRST-CLASS CRICKET MATCH AND A FULL INTERNATIONAL FOOTBALL MATCH FOR *SCOTLAND?*

4 IN 2018, SET THE *GUINNESS WORLD RECORD* FOR CLEARING A GAME OF *HUNGRY HIPPOS?*

5 WON TWO ALL-IRELAND SENIOR FOOTBALL CHAMPIONSHIPS PLAYING GAELIC FOOTBALL FOR *DUBLIN?*

6 OWNS THE HORSE *BROWN PANTHER* THAT WON THE 2015 DUBAI GOLD CUP?

7 FENCES AS A HOBBY WITH *WILL SMITH* AND *TOM CRUISE?*

8 SERVED AS AN EXECUTIVE PRODUCER ON THE 2009 MOVIE *"DEAD MAN RUNNING"*, STARRING *DANNY DYER* AND *50 CENT?*

9 AFTER MANAGING *READING,* BECAME A POSTMAN WORKING AT THE ROYAL MAIL SORTING OFFICE IN READING?

10 INVENTED A MOBILE DATING APP CALLED *"HOLA DATING"?*

11 PLAYED AMBASSADOR *PAUL DE FOIX* OPPOSITE *CATE BLANCHETT* IN THE 1998 MOVIE *"ELIZABETH"?*

12 APPEARED ON SUCH TV SHOWS AS *"CELEBRITY LOVE ISLAND"*, *"CELEBRITY WRESTLING"* AND *"DANCING ON ICE"*.

13 WON THE 60M SPRINT AT THE 2001 NATIONAL INDOOR YOUTH CHAMPIONSHIPS?

14 WAS VOTED OFF *"STRICTLY COME DANCING"* BY THE PUBLIC ON HIS 43RD BIRTHDAY AND ELIMINATED IN THE FIRST ROUND OF *"THE WEAKEST LINK"*?

15 TOOK UP MOTORSPORT AFTER RETIRING, WAS CROWNED 2013 FRENCH GT CHAMPION ALONGSIDE *MORGAN MOULLIN-TRAFFORT*, DRIVING A *FERRARI*, AND ENTERED THE 2014 24 HOURS OF LE MANS RACE?

16 SON OF A GRECO-ROMAN WRESTLING CHAMPION, WHICH STRIKER SERVED IN THE NORWEGIAN ARMY?

1001 ANSWERS

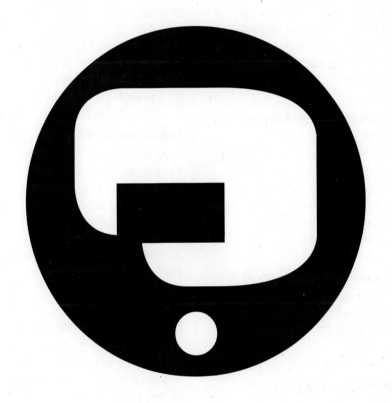

Fergie Time (pg 2)

1. St. Johnstone   2. Dunfermline
3. Rangers   4. Ayr United
5. St. Mirren   6. Real Madrid
7. Uruguay   8. 1990 FA Cup
9. West Bromwich Albion
10. Wine

Dortmunders (pg 4)

1. Adnan Januzaj   2. Ottmar
Hitzfeld   3. Henrikh Mkhitaryan
4. Real Madrid   5. Jovan Kirovski
6. Shinji Kagawa   7. Inter-Cities
Fairs Cup

The Reluctant Hero (pg 6)

1. Doncaster Rovers   2. Peter
Doherty   3. Ray Wood   4. Bolton
Wanderers   5. Bobby Charlton
6. Stoke City   7. Shrewsbury
Town   8. Swansea City   9. Crewe
Alexandra   10. Lou Macari
11. Carlisle United

Portuguese Imports (pg 8)

1. Sporting CP   2. Benfica
3. Sporting CP   4. Porto   5. Porto
6. Sporting CP   7. Guimaraes
8. Porto

Charity Cases (pg 10)

1. Queens Park Rangers
2. Swindon Town   3. Newcastle
United   4. Manchester City
5. Aston Villa   6. Liverpool
7. Tottenham Hotspur
8. Liverpool   9. Liverpool
10. Liverpool   11. Arsenal
12. Blackburn Rovers
13. Newcastle United

14. Chelsea   15. Arsenal
16. Chelsea   17. Portsmouth
18. Chelsea   19. Manchester City
20. Wigan Athletic
21. Leicester City

Nerazzurri! (pg 12)

1. Mikaël Silvestre   2. Ashley
Young   3. ŁKS Łódź, Barcelona,
Brøndby, Juventus   4. Alexis
Sánchez   5. Juan Sebastián
Verón   6. José Mourinho
7. Romelu Lukaku   8. Nemanja
Vidić   9. Diego Forlán
10. Laurent Blanc

Caledonian King (pg 14)

1. Sir Matt Busby   2. Sir Alex
Ferguson   3. Joe Jordan
4. Henrik Larsson   5. Gordon
Strachan   6. Jim Leighton
7. Jimmy Delaney   8. Andy
Goram   9. Pat Crerand
10. Gordon McQueen   11. Martin
Buchan   12. Tommy Docherty
13. George Graham

The Pint-Sized Terrier (pg 16)

1. Ian Callaghan   2. Alex Stepney,
Bill Foulkes, Brian Kidd, David
Sadler (and substitute goalkeeper
Jimmy Rimmer)   3. Wilf
McGuinness   4. Middlesbrough
5. Bobby Charlton   6. Harry
Catterick   7. Vancouver
Whitecaps   8. West Bromwich
Albion   9. Alan Ball, George
Cohen, Roger Hunt, Ray Wilson
10. 2020

The Dutch Master (pg 18)

1. Viv Anderson, Garry Birtles
2. Juan Mata   3. Ángel Di María
4. Fabien Barthez   5. Jimmy Rimmer   6. Bastian Schweinsteiger   7. Edwin van der Sar   8. Owen Hargreaves
9. Cristiano Ronaldo   10. Gerard Piqué   11. Víctor Valdés
12. Henrik Larsson

Latics Links (pg 20)

1. Denis Irwin   2. Paul Scholes
3. Charlie Roberts   4. Cameron Borthwick-Jackson   5. Gary Walsh   6. Andy Goram   7. Jack Rowley   8. Paul Edwards
9. Andy Ritchie   10. Albert Quixall

Fergie's Fledglings (pg 22)

1. Mark Robins   2. Wes Brown
3. Keith Gillespie   4. Darren Fletcher   5. Tom Cleverley
6. John O'Shea   7. Danny Welbeck   8. Jonny Evans

Harry's Game (pg 24)

1. Ray Wilkins   2. Laurent Blanc
3. Teddy Sheringham
4. Wayne Rooney and Ruud van Nistelrooy   5. Nani and Cristiano Ronaldo   6. Romelu Lukaku
7. Memphis Depay

POTY Potpourri (pg 26)

1. Ruud van Nistelrooy, Jaap Stam, Edwin van der Sar   2. Bastian Schweinsteiger   3. Henrikh Mkhitaryan   4. Laurent Blanc
5. Henrik Larsson, Zlatan

Ibrahimović, Victor Lindelöf
6. Cristiano Ronaldo   7. Carlos Tevez, Juan Sebastián Verón, Ángel Di María   8. Park Ji-sung

Deadly Dimitar (pg 28)

1. Bayer Leverkusen
2. Tottenham Hotspur   3. Hristo Stoichkov.   4. Carlos Tevez
5. Fulham   6. Monaco   7. PAOK
8. a) India

World Cup Winners (pg 30)

1. Bobby Charlton, Nobby Stiles, John Connolly   2. Laurent Blanc, Fabien Barthez   3. Kléberson
4. Juan Mata, Víctor Valdés
5. Bastian Schweinsteiger
6. Paul Pogba

Manager Macari (pg 32)

1. Bryan Robson   2. Noel Cantwell
3. Paul Ince   4. Sammy McIlroy
5. Mark Hughes   6. Gordon Strachan   7. George Graham
8. Johnny Giles   9. Joe Jordan
10. Steve Bruce

The Great Divide (pg 34)

1. Peter Barnes   2. John Gidman
3. Owen Hargreaves   4. Andrei Kanchelskis   5. Terry Cooke
6. Brian Kidd   7. Mark Robins
8. Andy Cole   9. Denis Law
10. Carlos Tevez

Centurions! (pg 36)

1. Peter Schmeichel   2. Tim Howard   3. Bastian Schweinsteiger   4. Zlatan

Ibrahimović   5. John O'Shea
6. Karel Poborský   7. Diego
Forlán   8. Nani   9. Javier
Hernández   10. Henrik Larsson

The Untouchable Flea (pg 38)

1. Memphis Depay   2. Alexander
Büttner   3. Daley Blind   4. Donny
van de Beek   5. Raimond van der
Gouw   6. Ruud van Nistelrooy
7. Jaap Stam

Debut-iful! (pg 40)

1. Dan James   2. Romelu Lukaku
3. Paul Scholes   4. Denis Law
5. Louis Saha   6. Ruud van
Nistelrooy

Globetrotters! (pg 42)

1. India   2. Azerbaijan   3. Malta
4. Azerbaijan   5. Netherlands
6. South Africa   7. India   8. Hong
Kong   9. Greece   10. UAE
11. Iceland   12. Hong Kong
13. South Africa   14. India

The Italian Job (pg 44)

1. AC Milan   2. Torino   3. Lazio,
AC Milan   4. Roma   5. Atalanta
6. Lazio   7. Lazio   8. Fiorentina
9. Sampdoria   10. Juventus
11. AC Milan   12. AC Milan, Verona
13. Fiorentina, Genoa   14. Roma
15. Juventus   16. AC Milan, Parma
17. Lazio   18. Juventus
19. Sampdoria, Parma, Lazio, Inter
20. Juventus

Red Devil Dragons (pg 46)

1. Clayton Blackmore
2. Wyn Davies   3. Billy Meredith
4. Dylan Levitt   5. Kenny Morgans
6. Ryan Giggs   7. Ron Davies
8. Mickey Thomas   9. Alan Davies
10. Daniel James

First Among Equals (pg 48)

1. Cristiano Ronaldo   2. Javier
Hernández (Chicharito)   3. Eric
Djemba-Djemba   4. Dimitar
Berbatov   5. Quinton Fortune
6. Kléberson   7. Juan Sebastián
Verón   8. Jesper Olsen
9. Nemanja Vidić   10. Arnold
Mühren   11. Eric Cantona
12. Diego Forlán   13. Carlo Sartori
14. Bastian Schweinsteiger
15. Andrei Kanchelskis   16. Falcao

Gone Gunners! (pg 50)

1. Henrikh Mkhitaryan   2. David
Herd   3. Danny Welbeck   4. Viv
Anderson   5. Ian Ure   6. Robin
van Persie   7. Mikaël Silvestre
8. Brian Kidd

The Early Bath (pg 52)

1. Antonio Valencia   2. Wayne
Rooney   3. Harry Maguire
4. Paul Scholes   5. Bastian
Schweinsteiger   6. Ray Wilkins
7. George Best   8. Roy Keane
9. David Beckham   10. Paul Ince
11. Marcos Rojo   12. Jonny Evans

Euro Kings! (pg 54)

1. Arnold Mühren   2. Peter
Schmeichel   3. Fabien Barthez

4. Laurent Blanc   5. Gerard Piqué
6. Víctor Valdés   7. Juan Mata
8. Nani   9. Cristiano Ronaldo

Ray "Butch" Wilkins (pg 56)

1. Chelsea   2. Dave Sexton
3. Mark Hateley   4. Paris Saint-Germain   5. Graeme Souness
6. Queens Park Rangers   7. Kevin Keegan   8. Watford   9. Jordan
10. Aston Villa

Rooney's Record (pg 58)

1. Romelu Lukaku   2. Cristiano Ronaldo   3. Robin van Persie
4. Javier Hernández   5. Dimitar Berbatov (tied with Hristo Bonev)
6. Alexis Sánchez   7. David Healy
8. Radamel Falcao   9. Denis Law (tied with Kenny Dalglish)
10. Henrikh Mkhitaryan
11. Sweden

Cardiff Connections (pg 60)

1. Fábio   2. Fraizer Campbell
3. Frank O'Farrell   4. Wilfried Zaha   5. Danny Drinkwater
6. Colin Gibson   7. Tom Heaton
8. Ole Gunnar Solskjær   9. Ravel Morrison

Turkey Travels (pg 62)

1. Kléberson   2. Robin van Persie
3. Rafael   4. Gabriel Obertan
5. Shinji Kagawa   6. Ronny Johnsen   7. Bebé   8. Radamel Falcao

Jaws! and the Jules Rimet (pg 64)

1. Jim Leighton   2. Tommy Docherty   3. Jim Holton, Willie Morgan, Martin Buchan (United), Denis Law (City) and Gordon McQueen (Leeds)   4. Lou Macari
5. Alex Ferguson   6. Gordon Strachan   7. Arthur Albiston
8. Andy Goram

"Life Is So Good in America ..." (pg 66)

1. Los Angeles Aztecs, Fort Lauderdale Strikers, San Jose Earthquakes   2. DC United
3. Chicago Fire   4. Atlanta Chiefs, Fort Lauderdale Strikers, Minnesota Strikers   5. Vancouver Whitecaps   6. Dallas Tornado
7. Real Salt Lake   8. Miami Toros, Detroit Express   9. Detroit Express   10. Los Angeles Galaxy
11. California Surf   12. Chicago Sting   13. Toronto Blizzard

Red Celebs (pg 68)

1. A Certain Ratio   2. Mick Hucknall   3. Kym Marsh
4. James Nesbitt   5. Will Mellor
6. Ian Brown   7. Usain Bolt
8. Rory McIlroy   9. Eamonn Holmes   10. Christopher Eccleston   11. Tony Wilson

Big Dunc and the Boys (pg 70)

1. Sir Bobby Charlton   2. Ray Wood   3. Harry Gregg   4. Jackie Blanchflower   5. Kenny Morgans
6. Albert Scanlon   7. Dennis Violett   8. Johnny Berry

9. Bill Foulkes

"The King of Kings" (pg 72)

1. Feyenoord   2. Wim Jansen, Jozef Vengloš, John Barnes, Kenny Dalglish (caretaker) Martin O'Neill   3. Cristiano Ronaldo and Diego Forlán   4. Arsenal   5. Frank Rijkaard   6. Zlatan Ibrahimović and Victor Lindelöf   7. Premier League   8. Barcelona

Crossing the Border (pg 74)

1. Henrik Larsson   2. Brian McClair   3. Roy Keane   4. Andy Goram   5. Dion Dublin

Outgoing Income (pg 76)

1. Southampton   2. Huddersfield Town   3. West Ham United   4. Derby County   5. Leeds United   6. Brighton & Hove Albion   7. AC Milan   8. Barcelona   9. Internazionale   10. Lazio   11. Paris Saint-Germain   12. Juventus

Captains Fantastic (pg 78)

1. Johnny Carey   2. Noel Cantwell   3. Bobby Charlton   4. Martin Buchan   5. Steve Bruce   6. Steve Bruce   7. Steve Bruce   8. Eric Cantona   9. Roy Keane   10. Peter Schmeichel   11. Roy Keane   12. Roy Keane   13. Gary Neville   14. Rio Ferdinand   15. Rio Ferdinand   16. Rio Ferdinand   17. Patrice Evra   18. Wayne Rooney   19. Chris Smalling   20. Antonio Valencia

Come Together (pg 80)

1. Brøndby   2. Beşiktaş   3. Oldham Athletic   4. Parma   5. Aston Villa   6. Newcastle United   7. Tottenham Hotspur   8. Molde

Dad and Lad (pg 82)

1. David Herd   2. Javier "Chicharito" Hernández   3. Jordi Cruyff   4. John Aston Sr.   5. Darren Ferguson   6. Steve Bruce   7. Gary Bailey   8. Andy Cole

Marching On Together (pg 84)

1. Eric Cantona   2. Peter Barnes   3. Alan Smith   4. Arthur Graham   5. Johnny Giles   6. Lee Sharpe   7. Jimmy Greenhoff

Baby-Faced Assassin (pg 86)

1. David Beckham   2. Stuart Pearson   3. Juan Sebastián Verón   4. Harry Maguire   5. Peter Schmeichel   6. Paul Ince   7. Carlos Tevez   8. Park Ji-sung   9. Mark Hughes   10. Chris Smalling

Carlito's Way (pg 88)

1. Real Madrid   2. Sporting CP   3. Lazio   4. Paris Saint-Germain   5. Sampdoria

The Boys in Green (pg 90)

1. John O'Shea   2. Johnny Giles   3. Denis Irwin   4. Noel Cantwell   5. Frank Stapleton   6. Kevin Moran   7. Paddy Roche

8. Tony Dunne

The Boys of '68 (pg 92)
1. David Sadler 2. George Best
3. Nobby Stiles 4. Pat Crerand
5. Jimmy Rimmer 6. Shay
Brennan 7. Brian Kidd 8. John
Aston 9. Bill Foulkes 10. Tony
Dunne 11. Alex Stepney
12. Bobby Charlton

Beckham's Bosses (pg 94)
1. Carlos Queiroz 2. Carlo
Ancelotti 3. Fabio Capello
4. Ruud Gullit 5. Preston North
End 6. Bruce Arena 7. Glenn
Hoddle 8. Steve McLaren
9. Fabio Capello

The Boys of 2008 (pg 96)
1. Fulham 2. Leeds United
3. Spartak Moscow 4. Monaco
5. Bayern Munich 6. Tottenham
Hotspur 7. Sporting CP
8. Everton 9. West Ham United
10. West Bromwich Albion
11. Internazionale 12. Porto
13. Sporting CP

From Ecuador to Wigan (pg 98)
1. Bobby Charlton 2. Keith
Gillespie 3. Tom Cleverley
4. Nick Powell 5. Steve Bruce
6. Michael Clegg 7. Darron
Gibson 8. Allenby Chilton

His Name is Rio (pg 100)
1. Lyon 2. Juventus 3. West
Bromwich Albion 4. Wigan
Athletic 5. Internacional

6. Everton 7. Roma 8. West
Bromwich Albion 9. Bayer
Leverkusen 10. Internazionale
11. Fenerbahçe 12. Internazionale
13. Arsenal 14. Fenerbahçe
15. Everton 16. Borussia
Dortmund 17. Dynamo Moscow

Rovers and Rangers (pg 102)
1. Ray Wilkins 2. Alex Forsyth
3. Andy Goram 4. Phil Bardsley
5. Roy Carroll 6. Jimmy Nicholl
7. Andrei Kanchelskis
8. David Healy

PFA Team of the Year: 1974-1989 (pg 104)
1. Martin Buchan, Stewart
Houston, Stuart Pearson
2. Gordon McQueen, Martin
Buchan, Steve Coppell, Joe
Jordan 3. Bryan Robson
4. Bryan Robson, Steve Coppell
5. Mike Duxbury, Bryan Robson,
Frank Stapleton 6. Bryan
Robson 7. Paul McGrath, Bryan
Robson, Mark Hughes 8. Bryan
Robson, Mark Hughes

"The Divine Bald One" (pg 106)
1. Marseille 2. Iker Casillas
3. Monaco 4. Brazil 5. Italy
6. Laurent Blanc 7. Paolo Di
Canio 8. Tim Howard 9. Linda
Evangelista 10. a) Aimé Jacquet
b) Roger Lemerre

Young and Gifted (pg 108)
1. Lee Martin 2. Ryan Giggs
3. Phil Neville 4. Wes Brown

5. Jonathan Spector   6. Giuseppe
Rossi   7. Federico Macheda
8. Axel Tuanzebe   9. Marcus
Rashford   10. Mason Greenwood

Top of the World! (pg 110)
1. Retired   2. Lyon   3. Queens
Park Rangers   4. Internazionale
5. Juventus   6. Queens Park
Rangers   7. Retired
8. Internacional   9. Real Madrid
10. Manchester City   11. Everton
12. West Bromwich Albion
13. Retired   14. West Bromwich
Albion

2010 Men! (pg 112)
1. Bastian Schweinsteiger
2. Gabriel Heinze, Ángel Di María,
Juan Sebastián Verón, Carlos
Tevez, Sergio Romero   3. Edinson
Cavani   4. Wayne Rooney,
Michael Carrick   5. Tim Howard,
Jonathan Spector   6. Serbia
7. Robin van Persie   8. c) Alexis
Sánchez   9) Kléberson
10) Carlos Queiroz

Meet the New Boss, Same as the Old Boss (pg 114)
1. José Mourinho, Chelsea
2. David Moyes, Everton   3. Sir
Alex Ferguson, Aberdeen   4. Ron
Atkinson, West Bromwich Albion
5. Louis van Gaal, Bayern Munich
6. Ron Atkinson, West Bromwich
Albion   7. José Mourinho, Chelsea
8. David Moyes, Sunderland
9. Ron Atkinson, West Bromwich
Albion   10. José Mourinho,
Chelsea

The Belfast Boy (pg 116)
1. David McCreery   2. Jonny
Evans   3. Jackie Blanchflower
4. Mal Donaghy   5. Jimmy Nicholl
6. Keith Gillespie   7. Roy Carroll
8. Sammy McIlroy   9. David Healy
10. Jimmy Nicholson

The Busby Buys (pg 118)
1. Alex Stepney   2. Albert Quixall
3. Denis Law   4. Pat Crerand
5. Wille Morgan   6. Johnny Berry
7. Ray Wood   8. Noel Cantwell
9. Harry Gregg   10. Tommy Taylor

Tommy Doc (pg 120)
1. Preston North End   2. Arsenal
3. Chelsea 4. Aston Villa   5. FC
Porto   6. Scotland   7. Dave
Sexton   8. Derby County
9. Queens Park Rangers
10. Wolverhampton Wanderers
11. Altrincham

The Doc's Discards (pg 122)
1. Brian Kidd   2. Carlo Sartori
3. Bobby Charlton   4. Jim
McCalliog   5. George Graham
6. Jim Holton   7. Denis Law

The Doc's Deals (pg 124)
1. Gordon Hill   2. Stewart Houson
3. Stuart Pearson   4. Mick Martin
5. Jimmy Greenhoff
6. Lou Macari

A Brace from the Ace (pg 126)
1. Liverpool (Milk Cup)
2. Sheffield Wednesday
(Rumbelows Cup)

3. Nottingham Forest
(Rumbelows Cup)   4. Aston Villa
(Coca-Cola Cup)   5. Liverpool
(Worthington Cup)   6. Wigan
Athletic (Carling Cup)
7. Tottenham Hotspur (Carling
Cup)   8. Aston Villa (Carling Cup)

Close but No Cigar (pg 128)
1. Gary Neville   2. Owen
Hargreaves   3. Nemanja Matić
4. Federico Macheda

Big Rom the Belgian (pg 130)
1. Anderlecht   2. André Villas-
Boas   3. West Bromwich Albion
4. Roberto Martínez   5. Marouane
Fellaini   6. Bobby Charlton
7. Antonio Conte   8. Diego
Maradona

Viva España (pg 132)
1. Real Madrid   2. Barcelona
3. Real Madrid, Sevilla   4. Real
Valladolid, Real Madrid
5. Sporting Gijón   6. Real Madrid
7. Barcelona, Celta Vigo, Alavés,
Espanyol   8. Osasuna
9. Villarreal, Atlético Madrid
10. Real Madrid, Sporting Gijón,
Rayo Vallecano

The Wee Man (pg 134)
1. Billy McNeill   2. Real Madrid
3. Ron Atkinson   4. Howard
Wilkinson   5. Ron Atkinson
6. Southampton   7. Martin O'Neill
8. Middlesbrough   9. Craig Levein

Brucey! (pg 136)
1.Norwich City   2. Trevor Francis
3. Sheffield United   4. Wigan
Athletic   5. Birmingham City
6. Hull City, Aston Villa, Sheffield
Wednesday

Fergie's Finds (pg 138)
1. Danny Wallace   2. Paul Parker
3. Dion Dublin   4. Ronny Johnsen
5. Jordi Cruyff   6. Teddy
Sheringham   7. Massimo Taibi
8. Louis Saha   9. Fangzou Dong
10. Michael Carrick   11. Owen
Hargreaves   12. Tomasz Kuszczak
13. Zoran Tošić   14. Chris Smalling
15. Phil Jones   16. Wilfried Zaha

The People's Choice (pg 140)
1. David De Gea   2. Gabriel
Heinze   3. Bruno Fernandes
4. Brian McClair   5. Roy Keane
6. Javier Hernández   7. Luke
Shaw   8. Ander Herrera
9. Antonio Valencia   10. Ruud van
Nistelrooy   11. Mark Hughes
12. Gary Pallister

Definitely a Keeper (pg 142)
1. Harry Moger   2. Jack Crompton
3. David Gaskill   4. Alex Stepney
5. Alex Stepney   6. Gary Bailey
7. Gary Bailey   8. Jim Leighton
9. Les Sealey   10. Peter
Schmeichel   11. Peter Schmeichel
12. Peter Schmeichel   13. Peter
Schmeichel   14. Peter Schmeichel
15. Peter Schmeichel   16. Mark
Bosnich   17. Edwin van der Sar
18. Edwin van der Sar   19. Ben
Foster   20. Tomasz Kuszczak

21. David De Gea   22. David De Gea   23. Sergio Romero

I'll Be Back! (pg 144)

1. Teddy Sheringham   2. Ashley Young   3. Garry Birtles
4. Arnold Mühren   5. Mark Hughes   6. Mark Bosnich
7. Nemanja Matic   8. Henrik Larsson   9. Les Sealey   10. Tom Heaton   11. Gerard Piqué

The Goalgetters! (pg 146)

1. Denis Law   2. Jack Rowley
3. Dennis Violett   4. George Best
5. Joe Spence   6. Ryan Giggs
7. Mark Hughes   8. Paul Scholes
9. Ruud van Nistelrooy
10. Stan Pearson   11. David Herd
12. Tommy Taylor   13. Brian McClair   14. Ole Gunnar Solskjær
15. Andy Cole   16. Cristiano Ronaldo   17. Sandy Turnbull
18. George Wall   19. Joe Cassidy

Golden Goals (pg 148)

1. Charlton (2), Best, Kidd
2. Morgan   3. Hughes (2)
4. McClair   5. Sheringham, Solskjær   6. Keane   7. Ronaldo
8. Vidić   9. Rooney   10. Rooney
11. Lukaku   12. Cavani

Young Guns (Go for It) (pg 150)

1. Peter Barnes   2. Mark Hughes
3. Lee Sharpe   4. Ryan Giggs
5. Andy Cole   6. David Beckham
7. Michael Owen   8. Wayne Rooney   9. Ashley Young

Lilywhite Links (pg 152)

1. David Beckham   2. Frank O'Farrell, Tommy Docherty, David Moyes   3. Bobby Charlton, David Sadler, Nobby Stiles   4. Francis Burns   5. Alan Gowling

PFA Team of the Year: 1990-1999 (pg 154)

1. Mark Hughes   2. Gary Pallister, Mark Hughes   3. Peter Schmeichel, Gary Pallister, Paul Ince, Ryan Giggs   4. Gary Pallister, Denis Irwin, Paul Ince, Eric Cantona   5. Gary Pallister, Paul Ince   6. Gary Neville
7. Gary Neville, David Beckham, Roy Keane   8. Gary Neville, Gary Pallister, David Beckham, Nicky Butt, Ryan Giggs   9. Gary Neville, Jaap Stam, Denis Irwin, David Beckham, Dwight Yorke

Mon Capitaine (pg 156)

1. Sandy Turnbull   2. Jack Rowley (2), Stan Pearson, John Anderson
3. David Herd (2), Denis Law
4. Stuart Pearson, Lou Macari
5. Frank Stapleton, Ray Wilkins Replay: Bryan Robson (2), Norman Whiteside, Arnold Mühren   6. Norman Whiteside
7. Mark Hughes (2), Bryan Robson Replay: Lee Martin   8. Eric Cantona (2), Mark Hughes, Brian McClair   9. Teddy Sheringham, Paul Scholes   10. Cristiano Ronaldo, Ruud van Nistelrooy
11. Juan Mata, Jesse Lingard

Atkinson Acquisitions (pg 158)

1. Remi Moses   2. Frank Stapleton
3. Garth Crooks   4. Paul McGrath
5. Colin Gibson   6. Terry Gibson
7. Laurie Cunningham
8. Peter Beardsley

Record Breakers! (pg 160)

1. Denis Law   2. Dennis Violett
3. Cristiano Ronaldo   4. Ruud
van Nistelrooy   5. Bryan Robson
6. Chris Smalling   7. David
Gaskell   8. Steve Coppell
9. Billy Meredith   10. Ole
Gunnar Solskjær

Record Makers! (pg 162)

1. Staus Quo   2. Andy Cole
3. "Glory, Glory Man United"
4. Stryker   5. Eric Cantona -
"Ooh! Ah! Cantona"   6. Martin
Buchan   7. "Lift It High (All About
Belief)"   8. Edric Connor

The Island Boy (pg 164)

1. Trinidad and Tobago
2. Graham Taylor   3. John
Gregory   4. Jimmy Floyd
Hasselbaink and Michael Owen
5. Blackburn Rovers
6. Birmingham City   7. Sydney FC
8. Roy Keane   9. Brian Lara
10. Katie Price aka Jordan

Unlucky! (pg 166)

1. Crystal Palace, Middlesbrough,
Nottingham Forest   2. Sheffield
United, Oldham Athletic, Swindon
Town   3. Manchester City,
Queens Park Rangers, Bolton
Wanderers   4. Sunderland,
Middlesbrough[e], Nottingham
Forest   5. Charlton Athletic,
Blackburn Rovers, Nottingham
Forest   6. Wimbledon, Sheffield
Wednesday, Watford
7. Manchester City, Coventry
City, Bradford City   8. West Ham
United, West Bromwich Albion,
Sunderland   9. Sheffield United,
Charlton Athletic, Watford
10. Reading, Birmingham City,
Derby County   11. Newcastle
United, Middlesbrough, West
Bromwich Albion
12. Birmingham City, Blackpool,
West Ham United   13. Wigan
Athletic, Reading, Queens Park
Rangers

Off to the Toffees (pg 168)

1. Morgan Schneiderlin   2. Tim
Howard   3. Phil Neville   4. Louis
Saha   5. Mickey Thomas
6. Andrei Kanchelskis   7. Darron
Gibson

Imported from France (pg 170)

1. Paris Saint-Germain   2. Monaco
3. Paris Saint-Germain
4. Monaco   5. Bordeaux
6. Monaco   7. Nantes   8. Paris
Saint-Germain   9. Bordeaux

"Second Means Nothing" (pg 172)

1. Aston Villa   2. Bolton
Wanderers   3. Southampton
4. Arsenal   5. Everton   6. Arsenal
7. Chelsea

Storming' Norman (pg 174)

1. Ron Atkinson 2. Billy Bingham 3. Pelé 4. Liverpool 5. Brighton & Hove Albion 6. Everton 7. Algeria 8. Everton

Turf Moor Teen Idol (pg 176)

1. Chris Eagles 2. Martin Buchan 3. Phil Bardsley 4. David May 5. Mike Phelan 6. Andy Cole 7. John Connelly 8. Luke Chadwick

England Expects (pg 178)

Sir Bobby Charlton, Ray Wilkins, Bryan Robson, Paul Ince, Rio Ferdinand, Wayne Rooney, Chris Smalling, Harry Maguire, Marcus Rashford

The Gaffers (pg 180)

1. Tommy Docherty 2. Ron Atkinson 3. Ole Gunnar Solskjær 4. David Moyes 5. José Mourinho 6. Alex Ferguson 7. Frank O'Farrell 8. Dave Sexton 9. Louis van Gaal

Deep in the Forest (pg 182)

1. Neil Webb 2. Ian Storey-Moore 3. Mark Crossley 4. Roy Keane 5. Peter Davenport 6. Garry Birtles

Working for the Man (pg 184)

1. Internazionale 2. Barcelona 3. Internazionale 4. Ajax 5. Paris Saint-Germain 6. LA Galaxy 7. Paris Saint-Germain 8. Juventus

PFA Team of the Year: 2000-2009 (pg 186)

1. Jaap Stam, David Beckham, Roy Keane, Andy Cole 2. Fabien Barthez, Jaap Stam, Wes Brown, Roy Keane, Ryan Giggs, Teddy Sheringham 3. Roy Keane, Ryan Giggs, Ruud van Nistelrooy 4. Paul Scholes 5. Tim Howard, Ruud van Nistelrooy 6. Gary Neville, Rio Ferdinand 7. Cristiano Ronaldo, Wayne Rooney 8. Edwin van der Sar, Gary Neville, Rio Ferdinand, Nemanja Vidić, Patrice Evra, Cristiano Ronaldo, Paul Scholes, Ryan Giggs 9. Rio Ferdinand, Nemanja Vidić, Cristiano Ronaldo 10. Edwin van der Sar, Rio Ferdinand, Nemanja Vidić, Patrice Evra, Cristiano Ronaldo, Ryan Giggs

Bafanarama! (pg 188)

1. Gary Bailey 2. Eric Djemba-Djemba 3. Wilfried Zaha 4. Manucho 5. Mame Biram Diouf 6. Eric Bailly 7. Odion Ighalo 8. Amad Diallo

In Hot Pursuit! (pg 190)

1. Aston Villa 2. Blackburn Rovers 3. Newcastle United 4. Newcastle United 5. Arsenal 6. Arsenal 7. Arsenal 8. Arsenal 9. Chelsea 10. Chelsea 11. Liverpool 12. Chelsea 13. Manchester City

Going for Gold (pg 192)

1. Gabriel Heinze 2. Cristiano Ronaldo 3. Sergio Romero and Ángel Di María 4. David De Gea, Juan Mata and Ander Herrera 5. Giuseppe Rossi 6. Dong Fangzhuo 7. 1908 8. Tim Howard 9. Bruno Fernandes 10. Rafael

You Little Red Devils! (pg 194)

1. Rio Ferdinand 2. Liverpool 3. David Beckham 4. Mickey Thomas 5. Mason Greenwood 6. David De Gea 7. Harry Maguire 8. Arsenal 9. Rock of Gibraltar 10. Carlos Tevez

Heroes and Villains (pg 196)

1. Eric Djemba-Djemba 2. Mark Bosnich 3. Stan Crowther 4. Ashley Young 5. Phil Bardsley 6. Axel Tuanzebe 7. Colin Ginbson 8. Ronny Johnsen

PFA Team of the Year: 2010-2011 (pg 198)

1. Patrice Evra, Antonio Valencia, Darren Fletcher, Wayne Rooney 2. Edwin van der Sar, Nemanja Vidić, Nani, Dimitar Berbatov 3. Wayne Rooney 4. David de Gea, Rio Ferdinand, Michael Carrick, Robin van Persie 5. David de Gea 6. David de Gea 7. David de Gea 8. David de Gea 9. Paul Pogba 10. Luke Shaw, Bruno Fernandes

Golden Boys (pg 200)

1. Teddy Sheringham 2. Andy Cole 3. Dion Dublin and Michael Owen 4. Dwight Yorke and Michael Owen 5. Ruud van Nistelrooy 6. Dimitar Berbatov and Carlos Tevez 7. Robin van Persie 8. Robin van Persie

Well, I Never ... (pg 202)

1. Zlatan Ibrahimović 2. Dion Dublin 3. Andy Goram 4. Axel Tuanzebe 5. Kevin Moran 6. Michael Owen 7. David Beckham 8. Rio Ferdinand 9. Neil Webb 10. Víctor Valdés 11. Eric Cantona 12. Lee Sharpe 13. David Bellion 14. Peter Schmeichel 15. Fabien Barthez 16. Ole Gunnar Solskjær

TRIVQUIZ

**FROM ABBA TO ZAPPA,
AMÉLIE TO ZULU, AND
AGÜERO TO ZIDANE**

**NEW FOOTBALL And POP CULTURE QUIZZES
EVERY DAY AT TRIVQUIZ.COM**

 trivquiz.com   trivquiz   trivquiz   trivquizcomic